DIVING
INTO
HEAVY
METAL!

DIVING INTO HEAVY METAL!

PHILIP KERR

Matador
Unit E2 Airfield Business Park,
Harrison Road, Market Harborough,
Leicestershire. LE16 7UL
Tel: 0116 279 2299
Email: books@troubador.co.uk
Web: www.troubador.co.uk/matador
Twitter: @matadorbooks

ISBN 978 1803135 502

British Library Cataloguing in Publication Data.
A catalogue record for this book is available from the British Library.

Printed and bound in Great Britain by 4edge Limited
Typeset in 11pt Minion Pro by Troubador Publishing Ltd, Leicester, UK

Matador is an imprint of Troubador Publishing Ltd

To Mum and Dad
Thank you for everything!

Contents

Introduction

'Hey, Phil, Phil! Wait there just a sec. I want to ask you something.'

There was urgency in Dave's voice. I had the feeling I was about to be drawn into something.

'Just a minute, mate. Let me get these drinks back to the table without any of them landing on the floor, will you?'

I 'excuse me'd through the crowded pub, with Dave in hot pursuit, and lowered the drinks tray delicately onto a table where two others were sitting munching something resembling peanuts. I didn't shed a drop. Years of practice. It's all in the bending of the knees.

Dave was right behind me now and was tugging on the sleeve of my T-shirt. There was clearly no way he was going to let me ignore him. 'There's something I want to ask you. I've asked the others and they're both working on it.'

Working on it...?

'Okay then,' I said, wondering what the heck he was going on about. 'Just let me sit down first.'

I sat myself down on a slightly wobbly wooden chair and got comfortable. 'Right then, Dave, spill the beans. What is it?'

Dave also sat down and looked at me intensely, in the manner of someone who was about halfway to being half-cut. 'Well,' he began, 'since you went up to the bar, the rest of us have been having a discussion. It's quite an important one actually.'

He'd thrown me the line, might as well bite. 'I see. I'm assuming you want to let me in on it?'

'That's right, yeah. We've been talking about death. Well, not really death. Not as such. More like funerals. We were talking about which track we would like to have as the last song before we, well, you know, get planted.'

'Planted?' Was he seriously talking about what I thought he was talking about?

'Yeah,' he went on. 'You know, goodnight, Vienna. The deep six.' His enthusiasm was slightly unsettling.

My pint stopped dead halfway between its beer mat and my lips. I froze for a while whilst I pondered the strangeness of the question and the suddenness with which I had been put on the spot. Why would I be asked a question like *that*? Was someone surreptitiously planning my demise? Would I be advised to take a taxi home tonight?

I was momentarily struck dumb. Where the hell had this come from? The group of us had just planned on having a few quick drinks to finish off the day, and now Dave was hitting me with prospective burial plans!

But, damn it, it was a good question. I took a swig, set my pint down again, and sat back, suddenly deep in thought. 'You know, I'm not really thinking about planning anything like that yet.'

Dave shuffled in his seat in order to address me a bit more directly. 'Yeah, yeah, that's fair enough. I get that. Neither am I. But if you were, what would your final send-off track be? It can be anything.'

I was stumped for a while. He was right: this actually was an important matter. Obviously, I didn't want to come up with something just off the top of my head. I was going to need a little time to burrow around in my memory and hopefully unearth a track with a particular resonance. And, obviously, one that the congregation gathered together would dig. Also, I would want to take St Peter into account. Upon being summoned through the Pearly Gates, I'd need him to know that I was there to party!

My eyes locked onto a small mark on the ceiling as I tried to clear my mind.

Funeral arrangements? The order of service for my final send-off? The soundtrack for my personal closing credits? Bloody hell! This was deep!

The question had led to a good deal of chin and head scratching around the table.

And then the others started reaching some conclusions. Jack looked up thoughtfully. He levelled his eyes at Dave. 'Yep, yep, I know, I've got it. I know exactly what I'd have. "Jump in the Fire" by Metallica. I think that one would suit the occasion very nicely. And that riff, wow, yeah. That's the one for me!'

A few appreciative and knowing nods later, Ania put down her wine glass and stubbed out her cigarette in the ashtray. A wide grin spread across her face, and she flicked back a strand of her long raven-black hair. 'What I want is "Body Bag" by Obituary. That would be just plain awesome! Death metal at a funeral. What could be more fitting?'

Eyebrows were raised all round. An impressive choice. Daring. Certainly very ballsy. The church hall in question would need some serious bass bins in order to handle that kind of low-tuned metal.

Meanwhile, I was casting around in my own head for something to suggest. I'd been listening to heavy rock and metal music since I was about eleven years old, and surely there had to be something lurking in there pertaining to funeral matters. But now that I had to single out a specific track through which a congregation would be required to reminisce on my earthly existence, I kept on drawing blanks. I took another swig of Żywiec. Dave, who was starting to get a bit hyper by now, was suggesting things like 'Never Say Die' by Black Sabbath, and 'Seasons in the Abyss' by Slayer. However, the rest of us decided that we had to collectively draw the line when he went completely off-piste and eagerly suggested James Brown's 'Get Up (I Feel Like Being A) Sex Machine'!

Then Jack and Ania started throwing other ideas around as well, all of which made good sense: 'Die with Your Boots On' by Iron Maiden; 'The End' by The Doors; 'Paint It Black' by The Rolling Stones.

There's no doubt about it: it's an interesting question, a real potboiler in fact. And it really does make you think. From the point of view of a heavy metal music fan, it makes you look back at your career as a participant in the genre, be it as a collector of records, cassettes, videos or CDs; as a band member or gig goer; as a T-shirt and poster collector; or, of course, as a maniacal and crazy-eyed dweller of the mosh pit! As anyone who knows me will attest, I've been stuck into my fair share of all of the above. The guys I was with on the night this conversation took place in a boozer somewhere in Eastern Europe were clearly of a similar mould. That's one of the things about metal fans: we tend to flock together, and we are quite forthright and very particular about our music. Over the years we've had to defend it against people pointing their fingers, laughing, telling us 'it's only a phase', or even castigating it as 'dangerous' and calling for aspects of it to be banned. As a result of this, we tend to develop fairly thick skins. This doggedness serves to make the true fans hold together all the stronger, and keeps us marching through, horned fists raised high, to the next gig!

Oh, and by the way, in case you're wondering – the track that I eventually hit upon that night? '(Don't Fear) The Reaper' by the Blue Öyster Cult. Very fitting.

A note on the text

As every true fan of heavy metal music will know, in the 1980s an organisation called the PMRC cropped up in the USA. The Parents Music Resource Centre, the bane of many bands' careers, sought to single out groups, or certain tracks they had written, and label them as dangerous: essentially, a menace to society. In short, they got in a lot of people's faces. They even published a list of tracks which they labelled 'The Filthy Fifteen'.

Well, that's bait enough for me. By way of riposte, I have also listed fifteen tracks (and in one case fifteen albums) at the end of each chapter. They simply represent the music that, for whatever reason, hit me the hardest at that particular point in my life. As it happens, some of those I have included featured on the PMRC's original list. So, to any members of that erstwhile organisation, happy listening!

CHAPTER 1

'Whoa, Hold the Bus!'

I've always been a foot-tapper. It's just something that's instinctively there. An innate trait, you might say. Well, that would make sense, because my parents are foot-tappers too. Maybe it's something in the Kerr genes. Very probably. But one way or another, my ears and, in quick succession, my feet (usually the right one taking the lead) seem to be instinctively drawn to a certain kind of music. It could be a subconscious thing, but somehow I've always felt as though I was 'down with the tunes'.

When I was about six years old my dad bought a radiogram. Now, anyone born after about 1980 will probably not have a clue what I'm talking about here, but the radiogram, in its day, was a serious piece of stereo equipment. It was, essentially, a big piece of wooden furniture on which you would play your records. On it, you could play LPs, 7-inch singles, and 78 rpm records. You could also stack the records on the spike in the middle of the turntable so they would automatically drop, one by one, in sequence. It had huge speakers on the left and right which spread the sound nicely around the living room. Some of my earliest memories come from listening to music coming out of that radiogram.

And my dad played amazing records. He had a massive collection, with the likes of Elvis Presley, Chuck Berry, the Beach Boys, Bo Diddley, the Shadows, and others all featuring in big numbers. But it was the singles I liked best. I had two particular favourites. These were 'Don't Bring Me Down' by the Electric Light Orchestra, and 'Mama Weer All Crazee Now' by Slade. Now, you try listening to those tracks and keeping your feet still. Good luck with that!

At that stage, I probably didn't even know what a guitar was. I certainly wouldn't have known how to associate a sound coming out of a speaker with a specific musical instrument. I may never have even heard the word 'guitar'. It is possible. But that crunching sound at the start of the Slade track, and the slamming bassiness of 'Don't Bring Me Down' had me crouched down on all fours and sticking my ears right up against the speakers. And I reckon that was the very start of my obsession with heavy metal.

*

One day, Dad took an album out of his cabinet. He called me over. 'Hey, Phil, I want you to take a listen to this. I think you'll like it. This is the Beach Boys. This one's called "Good Vibrations". See what you reckon.' He cued it up on the radiogram and rolled the big chrome volume switch up a few notches. The room was suddenly filled with strange high-pitched singing which seemed to float in the air. I gave Dad a 'hmm?' look. He then said, 'It's okay. Just listen, listen, any second now... There!' And then this sound flowed into the living room: *Chugga da chugga da chugga da!* Woah, hold the bus! What was that? It was suddenly all too clear what it was: Dad was air guitaring and giving it some Elvis Presley sneer.

Loud guitars, big choruses, and usually a bit of an instrumental break in the middle. That immediately became my fix, and I needed to get a lot of it, and frequently at that! The more out there the guitar sound was, the better. The tidiness, the precision, and the neatness of Hank Marvin was practically hypnotic to me, but something on the dirtier side always appealed more. One of the albums my dad owned was called *High Tide and Green Grass*. It was a Rolling Stones album. The Rolling Stones? Who were they? The record had a strange cover. The band photo had been shot using a fisheye lens, and one of the members seemed to have his hand in a cast. They actually looked like a dodgy bunch of hard cases! This wasn't just the usual photo of a smiling singer looking at you from the album cover and inviting you to have a listen. The Stones made it feel more like a dare.

And there were unbelievable sounds on this album. I have no idea how many times I had to reset the needle to relisten to the start of tracks like 'Nineteenth Nervous Breakdown', '(I Can't Get No) Satisfaction', and 'Have You Seen Your Mother, Baby, Standing in the Shadow?' Not only were these tracks loaded with attitude and aggression, they were dark and strangely menacing.

And what about *Tiswas*? Again, if you were born this side of 1980, you may have missed out here, but back then, *Tiswas* was required viewing for kids. It was basically Saturday morning chaos TV. The hosts were a very young Chris Tarrant and Sally James. A regular on the show was Lenny Henry, who would appear as Mr Razzmatazz the Rastafarian, David Bellamy the naturalist, and even as Trevor McDonald the newsreader. There was also Bob Carolgees. He would show up with Spit the Dog, who would simulate hawking up greenies and gobbing them at people. And of course, there was the Phantom Flan Flinger.

But the other thing that was fantastic about *Tiswas* was the music. They showed videos and held interviews with bands. It was on *Tiswas* that I first saw Joan Jett singing 'I Love Rock 'n

Roll', and The Damned playing 'Love Song'. I couldn't get those tracks out of my head. They are, in fact, still in there, alive and kicking and screaming!

As for *The Old Grey Whistle Test* though, that was a mystery to me. It was always on at about midnight, so I would have been tucked up in bed, possibly asleep. I was too young, so I never saw it. I was a wee kid who was still going to school in shorts and sandals. That sort of stuff was for the grown-ups. I was quite content with *Tiswas*, thank you very much.

But one thing was absolutely fundamental to me where music was concerned: it was *all about the guitar*. Whenever I was watching a music show and there were bands on stage, I would always look out for the guitar player to see what he was doing and how his playing shaped the sound of the track. The more it did, the better, so Status Quo and Eric Clapton, who were on TV a lot back then, were fuel for the fire. If, however, the guitarist was just playing some tame jingy jingy background stuff, then it was crystal clear to me, even then, that he was completely missing the point of having a guitar in the first place. The whole point of having a guitar was to be up front with it on the stage, to crank it up, and to blast it out as loudly as possible!

Right?

Right!

Blondie	'Hanging on the Telephone'
Chuck Berry	'Johnny B. Goode'
Derek and the Dominoes	'Layla'
Dire Straits	'Sultans of Swing'
ELO	'Don't Bring Me Down'
Free	'All Right Now'
Hoyt Axton	'Della and the Dealer'
Johnny and the Hurricanes	'Red River Rock'
Johnny Cash	'(Ghost) Riders in the Sky'
Marty Wilde	'Endless Sleep'
Slade	'Mama Weer All Crazee Now'
Status Quo	'Dear John'
The Damned	'Love Song'
The Rolling Stones	'Child of the Moon'
The Shadows	'Man of Mystery'

CHAPTER 2

'Just Listen to That!'

So at what point, you may ask, did the metal beast first bite me?

Well, it was actually in one of the most unlikely of places.

I ran into heavy metal music as a pupil at a catholic boarding school called Saint Hugh's College. Not the kind of setting in which you would expect to find teenage heavy metal fans communing in droves, far from it. But nevertheless, that was base camp number one. It was 1983, I was eleven years old, and I was a weekly boarder at this school.

The school itself was located just outside Nottingham in a village called Tollerton. It definitely wasn't the stereotypical private boarding school which some people will immediately picture in their minds, with money sloshing around everywhere, huge cars spread around the car park, and toffs walking around wearing bow ties and top hats. Not even close. Saint Hugh's was actually only a few years away from closing down, and at the time my dad was driving a white Lada Riva. Not the comfiest of cars, but it was affordable and built like granite with axles.

The classrooms for the first to fourth year pupils were more like portacabins arranged around a concrete car park rather than anything that looked genuinely permanent. We all filed into them after morning prayers and breakfast. We did the usual lessons: English, French, history, religious education, and such like. We also had to do judo and squash. I got quite good at squash, and even took part in one or two inter-school tournaments. I preferred squash to judo. I was a bit late putting on a growth spurt, which meant that I was very easy to throw around and flatten out!

My older brother, Andrew, started at this school a few years before me, and he was also a weekly boarder. Additionally, he was seriously tuned in to music. Every weekend, when Andrew came home, he would have a cassette that he had borrowed from a local library. It was through him that I first heard Bruce Springsteen's *Born in the USA*, Queen's *Greatest Hits*, and the *Freeze Frame* album by The J. Geils Band. These regularly got played in the car on Friday evenings when all the family drove over to the school to pick him up for his weekends at home in Derby.

Straight off the bat, I was fully into it. This music sounded incredible. Cool, in fact. There was a buzz to it, and danger; and also a sense of risk. After all, what would my parents have done if they'd found out that their little boy had been listening to an album which featured a track called 'Piss on the Wall'?

But I was fine with it, and that was a good thing, because when Andrew got back home, he played these cassettes a lot, and loudly, in his bedroom. I wasn't entirely sure what my parents thought about this, especially when he started hoofing out *Rattus Norvegicus* and *The Raven* by the Stranglers, but I was all in favour. Wow, that bass! To tell the truth, I had no idea what the Stranglers were singing about, but I had the distinct and instinctive feeling that these cassettes were not for parental consumption.

Then, one weekend, something happened, and it's still crystal clear in my memory. There are some things that remain etched. I was mooching about upstairs in the bedroom which I shared at the time with my younger brother, Robert. I was probably reading a book about dinosaurs, or the solar system, or a haunted house picture/story book, when my ears shot up, and my head with them. There was some kind of sound coming through the bedroom wall which separated Andrew's room from the one I was in. I say 'some kind of sound' because I really couldn't place it. It was shrill and screeching and seemingly unaccompanied for the most part. It was definitely guitar noise, but no images of Queen, Eric Clapton or Hank Marvin were springing to mind. Then, after the track had been playing for about a minute, the sound briefly stopped. If I'd been a cartoon character in a comic book, I would have been looking out of the page at the reader with a bemused expression on my face and a ring of question marks arrayed around my head: 'Wha…?'

After this brief pause, the sound restarted and got even weirder. It took on a style which sounded bizarre. To my primary-school-age mind, it seemed as though it could have been a church organ, cranked up to oblivion, playing an ascending scale pattern which climbed and climbed and climbed.

Something crazy was happening next door and it was really rattling my cage. I had to knock on Andrew's door. He invited me in. I probably did quite a lot of wild gesticulating and 'wowing', and then asked, 'What *is* this?'

'This is Van Halen. This guy is one of the best guitar players in the *world*!'

I needed to take in as much information as I could about this Van Halen thing, and as quickly as possible.

'Okay. Erm, who's Van Halen?'

'They're this band from America. They've just put out a track called "Jump". They're amazing! This one's called "Eruption"! Hang on, just a sec.' He ejected a cassette from his stereo, stuck a different one in, and fast forwarded it a bit to cue it up. 'Take a listen to this!' There was a brief hiss as the cassette started to play, and then the speakers blasted out a guitar crunch which actually sounded *hot!* It was as though there was genuine heat coming out of his stereo. What the hell was I hearing? There was a chugging, searing sound churning into the room. 'Yeah, this one's brilliant as well. This is called "Unchained". Just listen to *that!*'

My brain was in bits. Shot to ribbons. Completely frazzled.

It was absolutely clear that something was waking up inside me. I simply had to hear this band again and again. I was unaware of it, but Van Halen had been around since the 1970s and had released several albums up to that point. Fortunately, Andrew was absolutely into Van Halen and he often brought back tapes, or copies of tapes, which got listened to repeatedly, probably by the whole family such was his partiality for the volume switch. I remember Robert getting seriously into Van Halen as well. He still is!

But it wasn't until I went to this school myself that the penny dropped for real, and this was down to the guys in the second year, who just seemed to play music constantly. Even if you were nowhere near their common room or dormitories, you could hear it ripping out of their stereo. I think they casually left it playing whether there was anyone around to listen to it or not. Most of the time it was Motörhead or Judas Priest. That rang a bell, but I had no idea that it was tolling for me. Not yet.

I was wandering past the second-year area one evening, and for some reason they all seemed to be out. There may have been an evening class on that they all needed to attend. Possibly. Something like that. The routines in boarding schools could be pretty unorthodox sometimes. Either way, as I got to their area, I headed up the stairs and onto their main corridor. Strictly speaking, I was 'out of bounds' just on account of being there, and could have been due for a bollocking if I'd been caught. The cane was still used back then, and nobody wanted to get a whacking with that whipping stick if they could avoid it. I was unperturbed, however, due to the sound which had drawn me up there, as though hypnotised, in the first place. It sounded like metal music to me: the drums, the guitar, the very feel of the sound. No vocals though. It was all instrumental, so there was no chorus which might have given me a clue as to the title of the track. I listened all the way through to the end of it, barely moving a muscle. What exactly was I hearing? There was no question about it. I *had* to find out. There was no way I could accept not hearing that track again. And then the next one came on. This one was a bit more mellow, but still loaded with that feel which pushed all of my buttons. The singer was warbling on about a 'strange world' or something or other. The next one had more of a driving punk riff, but the one which came after that gave the game away. The title of this track was clearly 'Iron Maiden'.

So now I knew.

I realised that I'd been standing, statuelike, for about fifteen minutes before it dawned on me that I'd better get the hell out of there. I didn't want to get rumbled. I headed back down the stairs, furtively checking for any live-in staff who might grass me up and demand that I report to the headmaster for a clobbering. Nobody there. Good. I snuck away feeling slightly taller than before.

Then, sometime later, a cassette materialised in one of the first-year dormitories. I presumed it must have come from one of the second years. It was a C90 tape with an album copied onto it. Scrawled onto the side was 'Iron Maiden: *The Number of the Beast*.' That sounded like a great title. The Beast – Wow! It seemed to conjure up all kinds of images of monsters and vampires and misty graveyard inhabitants, and that suited me just fine. Having said that, I had no idea what the title of the album was actually referring to. There was an old cassette player knocking about, and I decided to borrow it. I put the cassette into the slot and clunked down the play button.

Well, that was it.

It was practically instantaneous.

As soon as the band kicked in with track one, I was completely transfixed! I sat there, cross-legged and with my mouth open, staring at the speaker. I couldn't believe it! I just couldn't get my head around the solid compact magnitude of this sound. This went beyond even Van Halen! The guitars were so intense and melodic, the vocals surpassed anything I had ever imagined, and the lyrics had a force and a power within them which drew me right in. This cassette didn't have a case, so I didn't know what any of the songs on the album were called, but I hardly cared. I was utterly mesmerised. There were tracks about Viking attacks, the American Indian wars, executions, and the Devil himself! My God! What was I listening to? This definitely wasn't the sort of thing I had been brought up on. But somehow, deep down even then, I knew I was going to be a fan of this kind of music. For life!

Well, finders keepers. I decided that the cassette was mine. I hid it under my pillow.

At the time, of course, I had no idea who Steve Harris or Dave Murray were, or even that this was the debut Maiden album for vocalist Bruce Dickinson. I didn't have a clue. But as it was, it didn't matter. And as for Bruce's scream at the start of the album's title track – *EEEEYYYYYEEEEAAAAAAAHHHHHH!* – what more of a call to arms did I need?

Alongside this, a lot of my pals were getting into a similar kind of thing. A friend of mine, Dominic, had got hold of an album called *The Last in Line* by someone called Dio. I was none the wiser, but judging by the album cover, this looked like metal of some sort. The cover showed a huge horned demon standing against a reddened sky with his fearful suppliants lit up beneath him. His hands were stretched out towards them as if he were issuing a diabolical command. Yes, this was a metal album, without question. On listening to it, I couldn't help but think, 'This is unbelievably fantastic!' It was distinctly different from the Maiden

I had heard, but certainly cut from the same cloth. The forcefulness of the vocals and the power of the distorted guitar riffs and solos put that beyond any doubt. The tracks 'We Rock' and 'Egypt (The Chains Are On)' grabbed me immediately. It was like taking a shot of musical adrenalin directly into the brain. I'd never had a wake-up call like this ever before in my life!

But again, I didn't know who Dio was. I had no idea that he had been in bands for years and that this was just his latest album. I knew nothing about his time in the band Rainbow with Ritchie Blackmore, Cozy Powell, and others. Also, I had never heard of Black Sabbath, and didn't know that Dio had fronted this massively important band from Aston in the West Midlands. I was only starting out on my journey, but I was all ears!

As Andrew and I were at the same school, I used to go up to his room from time to time to catch up, have a chat, and generally chill out. There were usually cassettes lying around, and two of his stood out to me: Saxon's *Strong Arm of the Law* and *Denim and Leather*. I'd never heard of Saxon. But judging by their album covers, they played metal and that was fine with me. That was exactly the kind of thing I was looking for. I duly borrowed them, copied them, and absorbed them riff by riff. The sound this band made had a meanness, a power, a drive, and a teeth-gritting energy which just spoke to me so loudly. That intro to the track 'Dallas 1pm': it stuck in my head as though with industrial glue. There was also quite a lot of Van Halen happening up there in the fifth form area. One of Andrew's mates was a certifiable addict.

Additionally, *Kerrang!* magazine had recently started up. As far as I knew, this was the only magazine on the press at the time which focused on metal music. Others, like *Melody Maker*, probably touched on it occasionally, but *Kerrang!* zoomed right in. If you were into metal, it was essential reading. It was also a brilliant way of discovering things you didn't know anything about. It was through this magazine that I first saw pictures of Ozzy Osbourne and Nikki Sixx. In fact, they were on the same page. The pictures had both been shot live in concert, and these two guys looked like fully fledged maniacs! For one, Ozzy, who had his shirt off, had a huge tattoo of a dragon around his neck. Sixx was brandishing (not holding) a jagged-looking black bass guitar at the crowd in front of him, as though he had some kind of evil intent. His hair was dyed black and spiked up like a punk, and he was practically covered in leather and studs. Who the hell were these guys? They looked batshit crazy! And for ages I thought these two were in the same band. I just naturally assumed that Nikki Sixx was Ozzy Osbourne's bass player. What a combination *that* would have been!

There were posters in every edition of *Kerrang!* and they were full centre spreads. They were normally shouted about on the front cover of the magazine and were a factor when considering a purchase. If the centre spread feature was of Megadeth pelting out something live during their *Peace Sells* tour, then all well and good. No qualms about that. If, on the other hand, a particular edition featured a poster of the Nelson brothers looking polite and pretty, I may have given it a miss that time.

Kerrang! posters made it onto my walls en masse. I picked up the magazine regularly and made additions to an ever-growing gallery. There were also pictures that just looked great within pages of text, and they had to be cut out and put up too. It was a meticulous business which involved concentration, scissors and a lot of Blu-Tack. This process was carried out with the utmost care and reverence. After all, you didn't want any ragged and jagged edges on your pictures.

My bedroom at home was plastered with posters and other pictures. The wall behind my bed was thick with them, with some corners overlapping others. And they could be of practically anyone deemed heavy. There was a picture of Jimmy Page playing this amazing-looking double-necked guitar. I didn't know any Led Zeppelin at the time. No problem: this guy looked like a god! On the wall he went, no question about it. There was also this band called W.A.S.P. which featured two insane-looking guitar players. One of them was playing a spikey white guitar with a Budweiser logo stretched right across its length. How cool was *that*? Also, naturally, there was my Iron Maiden calendar for 1986, which was loaded with pictures taken by Ross Halfin. Had this been a Christmas present, or had I bought it myself? I honestly can't remember. No matter though. That was the centrepiece. Every day of the year it was there. And every month the picture changed. It was brilliant!

Also, *Kerrang!* did album reviews. This was good, because you could find out who was who bandwise, how they were likely to sound, and how good they were. And the magazine had a unique way of quantifying quality: the 'K' system. It worked like this. Albums were scored out of five. If an album scored five Ks – a perfect score in other words – it was likely to be one that you would need to at least get a copy of. If, on the other hand, an album scored one K, this might not have been such a good bet, and would probably have been one to avoid. 'K' could be defined in differing terms from issue to issue. For example:

KKKKK: Kolossal!
KKKK: Kookin'!
KKK: Kreditable!
KK: Kritical!
K: Kowpat!

So you knew where you were!

I got to see occasional snippets of metal on TV at that time, but the main event for me came on Friday nights at ten o'clock. And this weekly event was the *Friday Rock Show*, with Tommy Vance. Vance was the genuine article when it came to rock and metal music. He really knew what he was talking about and made sure that this music got mainstream broadcasting rights on Radio 1. That was a major coup for fans like me, because, regardless of how huge metal was becoming as a global phenomenon, most DJs wouldn't poke it with a cattle prod back then. Vance would play new singles, promote albums, tell you who was on tour and when, and hold interviews with the likes of Toni Iommi, Dave Mustaine and Motörhead.

Fantastic!

Live on your radio!

Every single week!

I usually had to twiddle the dial on my radio alarm clock to keep the reception from crackling out, but back then that was just part of listening to any radio station. I did have to keep the volume low though. Strictly speaking, at that time of night I was supposed to be asleep. I reckon that on any other night I probably would have been, but these were Fridays, and Mr Vance had my full and undivided attention. It was on his show that I first heard 'Paradise City' by Guns N' Roses; had my first injection of Megadeth playing a live version of 'Devil's Island'; and had my initiation to Metallica and their latest single, 'Creeping Death'! Mr Vance's show was a lightning-rod for all rock and metal fans, and if like me you were a slightly green teenager, it was a gold mine that just kept on giving.

And then my time came. It was my birthday, and I was turning thirteen. All I was interested in was essentially heavy metal-based, so when Mum asked me, 'What would you like for your birthday, Phil?', the field was narrow and really quite simple. I put in a request. It was all I needed at the time. And when I tore off the wrapping paper that October, there it was in all its classic glory: my first ever metal T-shirt! I had definitely arrived on the scene, and now I had the gear to prove it. I wore that *Powerslave* shirt to shreds.

AC/DC	'Hell's Bells'
	'Highway to Hell'
Deep Purple	'Knocking at Your Back Door'
Dio	'Egypt (The Chains Are On)'
	'We Rock'
Gary Moore & Phil Lynott	'Out in the Fields'
Iron Maiden	'Phantom of the Opera'
	'The Number of the Beast'
	'The Prisoner'
Metallica	'Am I Evil?'
	'Creeping Death'
Saxon	'Dallas 1pm'
Survivor	'Eye of the Tiger'
Van Halen	'Eruption'
	'Mean Street'

CHAPTER 3

A Saturday Afternoon Pilgrimage

Every addict needs a dealer, and I found a handy one at close range.

In Derby's city centre there was a shop called Way Ahead Records. It was in a precinct next to the Eagle Centre, and was basically part of a red-brick 1960s bunker-like set-up, which characterised many post-war builds or rebuilds in British cities. One floor, maybe two, flat roofs, and square windows. Not the sort of place likely to find itself on many tourist routes, even for the most intrepid of visitors. There was an army recruitment office next door to Way Ahead Records, with pictures of men in camouflage gear pointing weapons at things seemingly in the near distance and just over your heads as you passed by. There were a number of other shops alongside and across the street: an Argos, various hardware shops, cafés and that kind of thing. There was usually quite a lot of litter drifting around as well. Aesthetic appeal was not in the blueprint when the city planners were working on this particular piece of urbanisation. And it showed.

Appearances aside, for young metal fans such as I, Way Ahead Records was the diamond in the rough. This shop had, in immense numbers, what most other high street record shops would apparently barely touch: namely, masses and masses of albums by heavy metal bands! Before even getting through the door, customers were enticed with full-sized album covers facing outwards towards them through the display window: Megadeth, Mötley Crüe, Judas Priest, Lita Ford, Accept… If you were into the scene, this was clearly the place to be. Upon walking through the door, the first thing you saw was stack after stack of records on the left-hand wall reaching way back into the depths of the building. There was also a smaller island of records just a quick step and turn from these which was set up in the middle of the floor. Beyond that, on the right-hand wall, CDs. There weren't so many of these, but then it was the 1980s, so they hadn't fully caught on yet. On the inside of the window with all the album sleeves, there were cassettes, stacked neatly and reaching up to eye level. I was about five foot three at the time, so you get the picture.

The great thing about this shop was that it didn't just sell mainstream metal. You could find Iron Maiden, Metallica, Motörhead, and Black Sabbath in there of course. But if you fancied trying out something a bit meatier, so to speak, you could delve into albums by young German bands such as Kreator, or Swedish ones like Bathory, or maybe you might have fancied sampling an up-and-coming band from California called Slayer.

There was always a reassuringly long-haired chap behind the counter, typically wearing a T-shirt which indicated that he was likely to be well versed in most of the music on sale at this store. And the music was always pumping! Way Ahead Records was a regular stop. It was my Saturday afternoon pilgrimage.

At the back of the shop, where it was a little darker, close to the fire exit, there were about half a dozen 10p video game machines. And I mean the older ones; so if you wanted to consider your purchases whilst playing Street Fighter, Splatter House, Spy Hunter or just plain old Space Invaders, and you had plenty of 10p pieces, you could mull things over whilst slicing up zombies or blasting aliens out of space. What a place to be!

Most of my early purchases, unsurprisingly, were made in Way Ahead Records. There weren't that many other places that sold the kind of thing I was getting into. So, I plunged in. I was in there most weekends, flipping through the album sleeves and running through the cassettes from A to Z. There were also seven-inch singles for sale. I picked up 'The Trooper', 'Aces High' and 'Two Minutes to Midnight' in Way Ahead. They cost me the princely sum of ninety pence each! Those were the days, my friend…

Way Ahead's clientele were a forthcoming crowd too. You could be going through a routine browse, and someone would probably come up to you and present you with an album sleeve for your consideration. In fact, that was how I got into Helloween. Some long-haired bloke just approached me and showed me one of their albums. He was a lively sort:

'Hey dude! How are you doing? Not seen you in here before.'

I was caught a little off guard. He went on: 'Looking at the Maiden stuff?'

'Yep.'

'You a fan then?'

'That's right.'

'Yeah, me too. And the rest of the world! Best band on the planet! Got a favourite album? Bloody love *Powerslave*! Genius mate, genius!'

A couple of years back, I probably would have said *The Number of the Beast*, but I'd moved on a bit since then. 'I'd say *Piece of Mind* at the moment. You know, "The Trooper", "Flight of Icarus", "Still Life". And "Where Eagles Dare". Instant classic that one. But then, you never know what they're going to release next, do you?'

'You're right there, mate,' the guy said, 'You're dead right. That logo' – he ran his finger across the top of the album sleeve I had picked out – 'badge of quality, mate, badge of quality.'

No argument there. I'd never heard it put that way before, but there was no way I could quibble.

He went on: 'Have you heard of this lot though?' He reached over to my left and took out a sleeve from an adjacent stack. 'Yeah, this lot are damn good too. I'd check 'em out if I were you.'

He held up the album sleeve right in front of my face. Interesting cover. I was sure that I'd seen it before, but I'd ignored it up until then.

'Yeah, this is Helloween. Not Halloween, *Hell*oween, right? This is really, really good. The guitar playing is fantastic! Really catchy stuff as well. If you like Maiden, you'll like this!'

The Keeper of the Seven Keys, Part 1 eh? Could be worth a try.

'Every single song is amazing,' he enthused. 'You can't go wrong with this album!'

All right. An interesting prospect. But not right now. I didn't have any cash on me at the time. But this could be a band to keep in mind. If they really were as good as this guy was saying, I'd need to dive in sooner or later.

He flipped the album cover over and showed me the picture of the band on the back. 'This is them. Most of them are about nineteen years old.' He then pointed to the singer: 'That's Michael Kiske. He's got an unbe*lie*vable voice. You've got to hear him when he lets it rip! And my girlfriend absolutely bloody loves him.'

'Does she?'

'Blimey, and don't I know it? I mean, if she got the chance, she'd do her best to jump his bones as soon as look at him!'

'She hasn't, has she?'

'Not as far as I know! After all, they're over in Germany somewhere, and we're cooped up in Derby, so I think I'm on safe ground.'

*

Way Ahead also had a bonus feature: it was a box office for buying tickets to metal shows and festivals, and it seemed to cover the whole of the UK. The arrangement was that when you bought your ticket, you could opt to add in bus transport to and from the location of the gig. Fantastic! What a brilliant little extra! The gigs were all advertised in the shop, and you just had to take a look at who was on the board for upcoming events. There could be anything from a show over at Rock City in Nottingham, which was just up the road, to things taking place in London or maybe even further afield in Scotland. You would buy your ticket, go to the relevant stand at the bus station on the appointed day (you never had any problem finding which one: all the hair and black T-shirts you see?), hop on the bus and sit back. You would then be taken to the venue, where you would slam away to Overkill or Exodus or Dark Angel, and then you would be brought home, battered and bruised but safe and sound. What a great system. Way Ahead's tag line for the service was 'You Rock, We Roll.'

*

There was a genuine feeling of adventure about getting into the world of metal, and Way Ahead was a portal for this. There was also a really steep learning curve. I was seeing albums by bands which I would never otherwise have even heard of: Angelwitch, Girlschool, Merciful Fate, Napalm Death… This was obviously not a scratch-the-surface-and-you-see-it genre, as seemed to be the case with commercial pop music. This was a study, and it went deep. There was a whole cave network of possibilities which offered any number of different routes for investigation. And there were so many avenues within this network: there was heavy metal; there was thrash metal; there was death metal; there was black metal… And these bands came from everywhere: the UK, the USA, Central Europe, Australia… Just about every single time zone and latitude was represented. It would certainly be true to say that the sun never sets on metal!

*

Of course, there were numerous other shops in which you could buy more commercial music. They used to be spread across city centres nationwide. The foremost ones were Our Price, HMV and Virgin Megastores. There were others besides, but these were the main ones. They would be adorned with posters of Madonna, Duran Duran (I actually quite liked them), and Wham! There would be 'Frankie Says…' and Kylie T-shirts for sale, and pop music trickling through the air. But, like George Mallory and his justification for climbing Mount Everest, you went to them 'because they were there'.

They generally had a metal section somewhere in their racks and they tended to cover the more popular bands of the time, so if you were looking for AC/DC or Black Sabbath you would probably not have had a problem. In fact, I bought my first official copy of Iron Maiden's *Number of the Beast* album and Ozzy's *Blizzard of Ozz* from the HMV shop (now sadly closed) on St Peter's Street in Derby. If, however, you had been looking for something a bit more left field, you might have run into one or two obstacles. Firstly, despite the fact that you knew full well that these less commercial bands existed, and that their albums had recently been released (you'd been checking in *Kerrang!*), there would be no evidence of them on any of the shelves in these stores. You could flick back and forth through the relevant initialled sections of the racks, but to no avail. These shops skimmed the nicely lit surfaces, but they did not plumb the more murky depths.

And then there was the question of the staff who worked in these shops. With all the best intentions, most of them didn't know an awful lot about the more shrouded musical subjects you wanted to discuss. It wasn't really their fault. After all, their main job was to sell commercial pop music to avid Radio 1 listeners and readers of *Smash Hits*. You would never expect to find any experts on bands such as Nuclear Assault or Sacred Reich in there. That was for a more specialised demographic.

I'll give you an example of what I'm talking about. Ever found yourself in this situation?

There was a band from Sweden called Candlemass. They had recently released an album entitled *Tales of Creation*. I knew this because I had seen an advert for it in the back of *Kerrang!* The album cover looked distinctly different from what would normally be expected from a metal band. It was instantly striking. It showed a biblical image from Genesis depicting an aspect of the seven-day Creation story.[1] This stood right out. I needed to find out what kind of sound accompanied this sort of imagery. I didn't anticipate cherubic choirs and pipe organs. According to *Kerrang!*, Candlemass played 'Doom Metal'. That was a new one on me. Curiouser and curiouser... The odd thing was that, on this occasion, Way Ahead Records didn't have it.

What to do...?

I went into my local branch of HMV and, having vainly trolled around the relevant racks, walked up to the counter. The chances are I was wearing a black T-shirt, probably with Iron Maiden or Megadeth plastered all over the front of it. Having waited patiently in the queue, I approached the short-haired chap behind the counter.

'Afternoon. I was wondering if you had an album in stock.'

'Okay then, mate. What is it you're looking for?'

'Well, it's by a band from Sweden, and they're called Candlemass.' (Telling the guy the band's nationality was probably beside the point, but I wanted to come across as an authoritative and informed punter.)

The store assistant's eyes glazed briefly, and then refocused.

'Candlemass?'

'Mmm.'

'Candlemass. Sounds like it could be something classical. Have

---

1   The cover of *Tales of Creation* was based upon 'The Creation of Light' by the French artist, Gustav Doré. Doré lived between 1832 and 1883 and, as I understand it, was an artistic child prodigy who never had a lesson in his life.

you looked in our classical department?' (Very probably I had. I used to, and still do, listen to quite a lot of classical music. A lot of metal fans do, you know.)

'Oh, I don't think so. I found the advert for the album in the back of *Kerrang!* you see. The album's called *Tales of Creation*. It was released a couple of weeks ago.'

'Ah, alrighty. I'll just have a quick look on the computer. Now, let's see...'

There was a bit of chin scratching, lip pursing and squinting concentration as the search on the green-screen computer ensued. The outcome, however, was fairly predictable. With a polite open-handed shrug and raised eyebrows I got my response: 'I'm afraid we don't have that one in stock in any of our stores. Sorry about that.'

'Not even in the London branch? Isn't there just one down there?'

'No, mate. They don't have it. As a matter of fact, Candlemass aren't even listed on our systems.'

I started to get the feeling I was heading up a blind alley. No joy here. Stumped.

But then a glimpse of possibility presented itself. The store assistant seemed to be considering something. He narrowed his eyes and said: 'But I could order it in for you. It might take a couple of weeks to arrive though.'

This was an option, and perhaps the only opportunity available to me aside from taking a trip to a record shop in Stockholm.

'All right then. If that's the only way, it's worth a try.'

I gave the assistant my home address and phone number, the landline number, of course: mobiles were still a thing of the future for me. I was then told that I would be sent a postcard in about a fortnight explaining that my order had been delivered to the shop and was available for me to collect. I thanked the assistant, who had actually been extremely helpful, and, with a sense of latent accomplishment, headed back out into the city streets.

On arriving back home, I explained to Mum and Dad that I

would be getting some post from the HMV shop in a couple of weeks, and exactly what it was all about. More metal! This wasn't a problem. My parents were getting accustomed to the stormy seas of my musical tastes. My folks, in short, were cool with it.

'So who are we going to be hearing this time?' asked Dad, whilst keeping one eye on the cricket. 'Maiden, AC/DC, or something else like that?'

'No, no. This is different. It's by a bunch of blokes from Sweden. They're called Candlemass.'

'Candlemass?'

'Mmm.'

'Candlemass. Never heard of them.'

*

And, of course, there were record fairs. These used to be held in Derby's Guildhall every few months, and if you were a music fan, they were like King Solomon's mines where the diamond seams were at their finest. You could get practically anything music-related at these fairs, and at rock-bottom prices. There would be limited editions, imports, picture discs, posters, cassettes, singles, signed bits and pieces. A lot of it was unofficial and bootleg (I think that was part of the point actually) and some of the cassettes had photocopied cards with grainy black and white images of bands on them. Who cared? Visitors to record fairs were eager customers and serious collectors, and money always changed hands.

Fairs like these were also great for picking up videos of your favourite bands in concert. These had usually been shot using some kind of archaic device from within a surging audience, so the sound and picture quality would normally be fairly rugged. But these gig videos, official or otherwise, were up for grabs!

That said, from time to time you ran into one or two things which genuinely did look a bit on the suspect side... So, there I was at the Guildhall in Derby, flicking through the 'L' racks of the rock/ metal section. Always lots of potential under 'L'. I was minding my own business, just casually browsing, when 'Urrrgh!' A couple of long-haired blokes snapped a quick look in my direction, as if checking to see if there was anything wrong with me. Just slightly traumatised, that's all. I had hit upon Led Zeppelin, and a live album from the late 1970s. This would normally be an agreeable prospect. However, the cause of my flinch had been the cover of the record. On it, and completely dominating it, was a black and white shot of Robert Plant on stage with his John Thomas protruding pendulously out of his jeans, and a dopy-looking grin on his face. Oh, erm, well. Perhaps not that one then.

*

We also had a family tradition. We kept this one going for several years, and still revisit it nowadays from time to time. During the Easter holidays the whole family would head off to North Wales for a week. We would stay in a little town called Criccieth, which is on the Llŷn Peninsula in the north of the country. Rather than lounging on the beach, our penchant was for walking. Every day, come rain or shine, we would plan a route on a Landranger map, sort out packed lunches and waterproofs, and get in the car to set off for the starting point. Over the years we climbed all over Snowdonia, and, although I don't want to start sounding like the tourist board, I really would recommend it!

Another thing we used to do whilst on holiday in Wales was visit a town called Porthmadog. It was a pleasant little place in itself, but it had a particular pull for all of us. This was a music shop called Cob Records. It sat right on the edge of the town, in the shadow of some beautiful Welsh scenery. It was an idyllic little location. Trips to Porthmadog always involved a browse in Cob, and this normally resulted in a number of purchases of second-hand cassettes. You found them at the back of the shop, and they would be stacked literally as high as I could reach. They stocked a plethora of albums, some of which were by more obscure bands. I remember picking one out. Rage: *Secrets in a Weird World*. Interesting sounding band. And there was a photo of three hairy guys wearing sunglasses on the album cover. The signs were promising, and this was a second-hand tape, so it was only about two quid. Cob's prices were always very much in favour of the buyer. It was also in Cob that I picked up my first copies of *Eliminator* by ZZ Top and *Lies* by Guns N' Roses. I also remember Andrew buying an album by Yes, *Big Generator* I think. He's always liked a bit of prog.

*

But of one thing there could be absolutely no doubt: it was much harder work being a music fan back then. More thought and effort needed to be put into following your bands of choice. There was no push button, instant gratification technology that gets taken for granted as the norm these days. There was no YouTube, no downloading, no streaming. The internet and websites didn't really exist in the way we understand them today. If you wanted to 'search' for information on a band or a tour, or on an album or single release, you had to go out and physically do the legwork. This might have meant going to your local newsagent and buying one of the music magazines; or it may have meant going to a local venue and checking the posters for the up-and-coming events; or it could have just been through good old-fashioned conversations with like-minded people. One way or another, it took effort and commitment. This was particularly the case with metal music. Quite often, although you knew it was out there, you felt like Mulder and Scully trying to prove its existence.

Complete Albums

Anthrax	*Among the Living*
Candlemass	*Tales of Creation*
Dark Angel	*Darkness Descends*
Iron Maiden	*Iron Maiden*
	Live After Death
King Diamond	*Them*
Kreator	*Coma of Souls*
	Extreme Aggression
Megadeth	*Peace Sells (But Who's Buying?)*
	So Far, So Good – So What!
Metallica	*Master of Puppets*
	Kill 'Em All
Slayer	*Reign in Blood*
	Show No Mercy
Van Halen	*1984*

CHAPTER 4

Incendiary music

I was like a bloodhound.

I wanted to sniff out whatever I could find that would add to my growing metal collection. Clearly, there were hundreds of bands out there, and most of them had released several albums already. But which ones should I target? I only had limited spending power, and some of that usually found its way into the Space Invaders machine at Way Ahead. But, as it turned out, I was in luck. Whilst in the 1980s the pop scene was being promoted through the *Now That's What I Call Music* collections, the metal scene had a similar thing going on. It wasn't as blatantly plugged, but if you did a bit of digging, it was surprising what you could unearth. I wasn't particularly fussy at the time and was generally open to whatever.

So I started digging.

The first metal collection I bought was, ironically, not even for me. It was actually a present for my younger brother, Robert. It came out in 1986 and was called *Masters of Metal*. Not the most creative of titles, granted, but the album did what it said on the sleeve. It was fairly mainstream for the genre, and the bigger bands of the time featured on it. Iron Maiden got things underway with 'The Trooper'. Well, that's a great way to start any album. Straight to the sirloin! Then there were tracks by the likes of the Scorpions, Dio, Manowar, and Rush. This was painting with a pretty broad brush, but it all gelled very nicely. I'm not sure if Rob had been into this kind of music at the time, or if it was just a blatant exercise in indoctrination on my part, but he played it a lot, and went all about the place bellowing, 'STAND UP AND SHOUT!' and 'HEAVY METAL DAZE!'

It didn't take long before I realised that picking up compilation albums was a simple, and quite cheap, way of sampling as many different morsels of metal as possible. So I went out specifically looking for them.

Whilst browsing in WH Smiths in Derby one weekend, I found a cassette. There was a picture of a guitar on it. A red Flying V. This looked interesting, and instinct kicked in. Naturally, it found its way home with me. It had the not particularly inspiring title *Time to Rock*. Oh well, cheesiness aside, the track listing looked quite appealing. There were tracks by Mötley Crüe (okay, heard of them); Tesla (who?); Testament (oh yes, that was thrash); and Guns N' Roses (that rang a bell. I'd heard they were of some interest in America).

Back at home, I loaded the cassette into my stereo. This album couldn't have been more varied if it had tried. It kicked off with Mötley Crüe doing a version of 'Jailhouse Rock' which may have had Leiber and Stoller doing pirouettes in their graves. It also left me stunned, but not necessarily for the right reasons! So, onwards. Faster Pussycat and 'Bathroom Wall'. This was basically a track about the band's lead singer and his adventures with a woman who had left her phone number on a bog wall somewhere, with the promise of a good time offered to those who called it. The phone number was even quoted in the track!

I wasn't really sure about the way things were panning out. Up to this point, *Time to Rock* had comprised a mangled classic and a track about toilet trading!

So far, so bloody odd.

I did a little fast forwarding. And then I found Metal Church and their track 'Start the Fire'. This had been recorded live at the Hammersmith Odeon in London and was much more like it. There was nothing showy or glitzy here: this was no-nonsense, straight to the point stuff. There was a chugging engine behind Metal Church's music which was dark and pounding and relentless. Their track needed to be heard again! And it was. I rewound it several times before I moved onto the next one. And that was Manowar, 'Fighting the World'. Things were looking up. Guns N' Roses also sounded okay. Their vocalist was a bit on the shrill side though. Testament, on the other hand, sounded great. The guitar playing was in a different league, and the solo was a belter! Their track, 'Burnt Offerings', was the first thrash metal track I ever paid any attention to. This was definitely the start of something for me. A seed had been sown.

Searching out music like this was a good thing, because there was a compilation series which ran for several volumes from the 1980s and into the early 1990s. I had some of these on cassette as well. (I generally preferred cassettes as I had a Walkman. If this music was portable, that made it even better!) These collections were entitled *Speed Kills*. They were, unsurprisingly, entirely thrash-based. Young American bands such as Exodus, Metallica and Megadeth featured here; as did British bands like Onslaught, Re-Animator, and Acid Reign. European bands were also represented: Turbo from Poland, Celtic Frost from Switzerland, and Destruction from Germany. It was a mixed bunch, and the net was cast far and wide. A good, good springboard!

And then there was Noise.

Noise was a record label which was based in Germany. It was set up in the mid-1980s with the principal intention of promoting European thrash metal bands. The scene in Europe was still an emerging and relatively obscure phenomenon at this point, and a lot of young bands, mostly crewed by teenagers, needed a break. Noise helped to provide an outlet for them. Fortunes were mixed over the years with sales rising and falling and band members coming and going, (and sometimes coming back), but some bands such as Kreator, Helloween, and Gamma Ray made a lasting impression and still fill good sized venues to this day.

And Noise also released compilations.

One weekend I was in Way Ahead Records with my usual pocketful of 10p pieces, when I chanced across an album cover which looked so cool I couldn't pass it by. The cover art was tinged with red, and it showed a view through an arched window. A caped figure, with his hands drawn together as though in prayer, was bowing into the image from the right. However, there was something red dripping from his grip, and his fingernails looked sinisterly elongated. This album was entitled *Doomsday News: The New Generation of Heavy Metal*, and it was released in 1988.

I took it out of the rack and stared at the cover for a while. This looked like nothing else I had ever seen. Talk about dark! And it was a gatefold album, which made it even better. I piled up my pocketful of 10p's on the counter and sealed the deal.

Doomsday News was a collection which I obsessed over. Not only was the artwork unbelievable, the music that exploded out of the speakers when I put the needle down was of a totally different type to anything I'd heard before. There was an intensity to these tracks. They were technical, complicated, and the playing was relentless. The melodies ricocheted back and forth amongst incredibly tight and intricate rhythm sections, and this elevated the feel of the sound to an even greater height. I shan't run through it track by track (it's worth hunting a copy down and enjoying it for yourselves), but some bands unquestionably deserve a mention.

Scanner's opener, 'Galactos', was a barnstormer! There was no subtle introductory section, no suggestion that you might need to strap yourself in. It was an immediate and direct attack, but it was loaded with melody all the way through, and had an incredible solo in the middle. What a start!

Track four, 'Arrogance in Uniform', was by a Swiss trio called Coroner. I've got to admit, this one took a bit of listening to. There was just so much going on that it was difficult to take it all in right away. This was a track that definitely made me do a double take. Before even getting to the main riff section there was an intro which sounded so complicated that it felt like a scorching blur. All the way through there were flurries of guitar solos flying around that I think would even have had Eddie Van Halen scratching his head. And the actual solo in the middle of the track was so controlled, so perfected, so precise. The guitarist used the two-handed tapping technique, but not in a way I had ever heard it used before. This was practically incendiary music!

Then, on side two, there was a switch of tone. If anything, things started to sound a little, well, happier. What was going on now? It turned out that I'd just bumped into Helloween and their track 'I'm Alive', and these guys from Hamburg sounded like life coaches. The lyrics were all about positivity and friendship and the love of life. *Eh?* The Four Horsemen of the Apocalypse had clearly dropped out of the equation here. Helloween was not at home to that particular quartet! In my, admittedly, limited experience, metal music normally came with an implicit menacing snarl in its tone. *GRRRRRR!* Not here though. This actually felt quite uplifting. I could make out all of the lyrics, and, if anything, the guitar solos almost sounded cheeky. It feels strange putting that down in writing, but give it a listen and see what you think.

Some of the other bands which featured on this compilation were Kreator, Tankard, Vendetta and Sabbat. With just one track each, they all brought something to the party which had a spicier kind of bite to what I had been used to. There was no sign of Ozzy, Maiden, Saxon, or Motörhead to be found here. The tracks on *Doomsday News* all shot off at crazy tangents. It was staggering!

I was absolutely amazed at how good this album was. For a long time, *Doomsday News* was all I would listen to. It was like a musical artillery rampage, but there was nothing scrappy or trashy about it at all. It was a meticulous musical assault, and the playing was stunning! And the three or four-minute snippets of these obscure new-found bands taught me a lesson that I still abide by today: always look beyond what you know. You never know what gems you may find out there. Just because many metal bands are not huge sellers or household names, that hardly means that they may not be amazing in and of themselves. Plumb the depths and find the diamonds. That's the way to do it!

But then something, which I don't think had ever happened to me before, happened. I was in the living room at home, and I had *Doomsday News* hoofing out of the stereo. (I should add that my parents were out at the time. I don't think they would have been in favour of the seismic tremors I created with this album when I was by myself.) Deathrow were just pounding through their track, 'Scattered by the Wind', when: DAMN IT, BASTARD, *FUCK!*

The needle skipped!

It was right after the guitar solo, as the riffs were building up to the massive climax of the track, when – clunk, clunk, clunk...! That repeated spin of the album kept coming back, over and over and over again! Oh Christ, no! NO! *NOT THIS!* With extreme care, I lifted the needle from the record's surface and delicately replaced it at a slightly earlier point in the track. I listened again, with almost panicked attention, and let the track play whilst willing, compelling, exhorting the needle to follow the groove and stay neatly nestled in its place. After all, that was what it was supposed to do, wasn't it? Just be good and do your job. *Pleeease!* I got right down to eye level with the groove and the needle and watched, frozen, as it approached the offending section. And then... clunk, clunk, clunk!

What the hell was I going to do? One of the key tracks on the album was knackered! And the more I tried to play it, the more knackered it was likely to become! Moments earlier, metal had been pouring joyously out of the speakers and I had been headbanging and air guitaring like a loon. Now there was an eerie stillness in the living room.

The music had died.

Shit!

I had to somehow replace this album. It was one of the cornerstones of my collection. It couldn't just break and cease to exist. No way, no how.

I was never a particularly good keeper of receipts, and the likelihood of owning one for my purchase of *Doomsday News* was about odds on with Mike Tyson signing up for an elementary course in crochet. Slim at best. So I headed back down to Way Ahead to see if there was another copy on the shelf. No, there wasn't. Was it available on cassette? Certainly not as far as I could see. What about on CD? My hopes lay there, as CDs were the emerging media for listening to music.

I spoke to the guy behind the counter and asked him if he knew the album. More importantly, was there another one in stock? He checked but told me that it had only been released on a limited run and only on vinyl. In other words, it was no longer available.

The trail had run cold. I was, as they say, shit out of luck!

As far as I could see, the only thing I could do was try to locate any albums by the bands I had found out about on my now broken record. After all, when life deals you lemons you've got to know what to do with them.

So, I started digging again.

I got back to the record and cassette stacks.

I had mixed success, but I think I did fairly well. Some of the bands appeared to be genuinely very obscure, and their albums were difficult to find anywhere. On the other hand, I had no trouble finding a copy of Helloween's *Keeper of the Seven Keys, Part 1*. That guy I'd bumped into in Way Ahead a while back had been right – this album was a corker! I was able to pick up a copy of *Raging Steel* by Deathrow, which contained the track which had conked out on my compilation. I also managed to find a copy of *Terrible Certainty* by Kreator, which contained the track 'Toxic Trace'. This was probably the speediest and most violent album I had ever heard at the time. God, it was *mad*! It seemed to be an unleashing of utterly unrestrained savagery. I've got to say that, back then, it was a bit too much! The vocals sounded like they were coming out of a Ringwraith, and the drumming sounded like a bombing raid! The guitar solos exploded at you, with whammy bar harmonics being wrenched way out of key at almost every opportunity. I needed to let this one grow on me for a while. And I did.

Of course, you weren't entirely restricted to official compilation releases. You could also make your very own compilations. The HMV shop used to sell C90 cassettes in batches of ten. With these you could copy forty-five minutes of tracks on each side, and you could fill up the time with anything you wanted. Basically, all you needed was a cassette player with a record button. You would play the album you wanted to copy, either a record or tape, in a hopefully vacant room, whilst the C90 spooled around in the recorder with its play and record buttons pressed down. The tape would record the sound in the room. You could record complete albums, or individual tracks from them, and create a personalised playlist. The sound would usually be a bit muffled and scratchy, but at least it was an impression of the music you were after. If you had a double cassette deck with high-speed dubbing that was even better, because it was faster and it was all done within a single machine. This gave you a much better sound. C90s were also very useful for recording the *Friday Rock Show*.

I made dozens of collections, and practically drilled them into my brain courtesy of my Walkman. Occasionally, I even managed to convince my dad to play them on the car stereo. Occasionally.

Accept	'Fast as a Shark'
Anthrax	'Gung-Ho'
Black Sabbath	'War Pigs'
Dio	'Stand Up and Shout'
Hanoi Rocks	'Tragedy'
Helloween	'I'm Alive'
Iron Maiden	'The Trooper'
Malice	'License to Kill'
Metal Church	'Start the Fire'
Onslaught	'Fight with the Beast'
Rainbow	'All Night Long'
Rush	'Spirit of Radio'
Saxon	'Princess of the Night'
Scanner	'Galactos'
Testament	'Burnt Offerings'

CHAPTER 5

Points and spikes

Now, I'm absolutely certain that this happens the world over and on every single continent, with the possible exception of Antarctica. There comes a stage in teenagers' lives, particularly in the case of budding metal music fans, when they develop a compulsion. It appears quickly, as though overnight, and fully formed. MUST HAVE A GUITAR! Listening was all well and good, and jumping around on a bed whilst shredding out solos on a squash racket was fine, but I had to be more than just an observer. I needed to be a part of this music.

On the other hand, to many parents a teenager with a guitar can be an ominous prospect, because if said teenager gets said guitar and they bond, they could pretty much bank on homework going straight out of the window. But I asked for an acoustic guitar for Christmas in 1985 and was genuinely over the moon when I unveiled my present from Mum and Dad: my very first six-string! This was a thing of beauty. My ticket to becoming a rock god. I'd nail *Eruption* in no time. Just try and stop me!

Having said that, at the time I didn't really understand the difference between an acoustic guitar and a classical guitar. If anything, I probably thought they were basically the same thing, and my mum and dad probably did too. You didn't plug them in, and they had holes in the middle of their bodies. That was to let the sound come out. That meant acoustic, right? Well, yes and no. What I had been bought was, in fact, a classical guitar with three metal strings and three nylon strings – not an acoustic at all. I didn't know any different, and to be perfectly frank, I couldn't have given a toss! I was tooled up and ready to shred!

Not that I had any clue what to do with it. For starters, tuning it up was interesting. My naive mind just assumed that guitars were naturally in tune (after all, they were always in tune in the shops), and that there was no need for any human intervention in this regard. Not the case. I had to go down to my local music shop and buy a tuning fork. There wasn't much in the way of electronic tuners on the market back then, and they were viewed as a bit slapdash at the time. If you haven't used a tuning fork, and let's face it, they are generally viewed as museum pieces these days, they worked like this. What you basically had was a thin piece of metal about four inches long. It had a stem, which you held, that split into two smaller parallel prongs. You had to take hold of the stem and then whack the branches on your knee. Next you needed to place the bottom of the stem on a hard surface and hold it upright. The thing would ring out with a tone held in the vibration. This particular fork was tuned to an 'A' note. And that was a start, because I knew that the second thickest string on the guitar was an A. I just needed to wiggle the relevant peg at the end of the neck and get it up to pitch. I was getting somewhere!

Now all I had to do was learn how to play it.

I had been learning to play the piano, but to be honest it didn't really float my boat. In plain terms, it bored me rigid. I think this had a reciprocal effect on my teacher. She didn't exactly jump for joy when I turned up for lessons. I absolutely got that being able to play the piano could be a really groovy thing, and I'd heard some of my dad's Fats Domino and Little Richard records. All good. Loved them then, love them now. But most of my lessons seemed to be spent practising scales and broken chords. And exasperating my teacher, because, in all honesty, *A Tune A Day Book One* did not inspire me with anything resembling a creative muse. Also, she wasn't what you could call encouraging. When I made a mistake, which was often, she would puff out her somewhat chubby cheeks and grab my hands, placing them on the keyboard where they needed to be. This was a bit off-putting for a number of reasons.

'You're doing it *wrong* again!'

'Oh for goodness' *sake. Watch* me!'

'Are you paying attention to *anything* I'm showing you?'

What did she expect? I was a fairly uncoordinated teenager, hardly the new Vladimir Ashkenazy. I wasn't even up to Grade One! Maybe one of the reasons I kept hitting the wrong notes was because, rather than looking at the page of music in front of me, I kept glancing down at my watch to see how much longer I had to continue with this pursuit. God, this was a dull business!

I needed to drop this ebony and ivory cobblers and start playing something that actually interested me. And that was metal. So I did the right thing: I ditched the piano and switched to guitar. Shortly afterwards, I met my first guitar teacher, a Mr Baxter. He was quite a pleasant chap: specs, a short-cropped beard, and always a collar and tie. The lessons were held in one of the boarding school's assembly rooms, which had wood-panelled walls and a high ceiling. Good for acoustics I shouldn't wonder. But I don't think I was quite what Mr Baxter had anticipated.

He was, understandably, surprised when I strolled into my first lesson packing an absolutely bottom of the range classical guitar and an Iron Maiden *Number of the Beast* songbook! I don't suppose he'd been banking on that. He'd probably been expecting someone with a bit more finesse and delicacy. Well, for his sins, he got me. God alone knows how he described me to his missus when he got home! He asked me what I was interested in learning to play, as if it hadn't been made absolutely clear by what I had brought with me to the lesson. I opened the book at *Hallowed Be Thy Name*. This was one of my favourite tracks by anyone at the time. I had the distinct feeling that Mr Baxter hadn't heard of it though. Shame. He'd been missing out. I'm not sure what put him off more: the fact that I wasn't at all interested in learning to play Rodrigo, or the lyrics of the track which were written under the staves!

So, as history would have it, the first melody I ever learned to play was to the tune of Bruce Dickinson screaming out the verse about the priest and the last rites. Ten plucks rotating around three notes. Yeah! I was playing metal! We played this part over and over, stretching basically between the seventh and fifth frets. Not only was I playing something I liked, I was playing up the neck of the guitar, which doubled the level of cool. Now *that's* what I call a music lesson! After that half-hour session, I felt like I was about seven feet tall. The fingertips on my left hand were a bit sore, but that hardly bothered me. Over the next few weeks, we worked out the tunes to some of the other tracks in my book. The melody of *Run to the Hills* was tricky and involved some serious finger stretches, but I soldiered on through it.

At the weekends, when I was at home, I practised in my room day and night plinking and plonking away, looking at my right hand, looking at my left hand, looking at the notes, and working it all out. I think my parents assumed I'd become a hermit, they saw me so rarely.

It didn't really sound right though, did it? No, not really. Actually, it didn't sound anything like the real thing, and that was a pity because I knew I was playing the right notes. My slightly bemused teacher had shown me which frets I needed to put my fingers on. I'd put little coloured stickers on them to help me remember. I spent hours banging away on my guitar in my dormitory room at school, probably pissing my bunk mates off a bit, just trying to get that edge into the sound. But for all the righteous endeavour and sore fingertips, it wasn't coming across. It was glaringly obvious why: my guitar had a hole in the middle. That's not metal! I needed something electric, solid, and with as many pickups as could be crammed between the bridge and the top fret. I knew the kind of thing. I'd recently seen an absolutely insane-looking band called Venom on a TV show called *ECT*. Their guitarist was chucking around something that looked like a black battleaxe. It was solid with pickups. That was the one I required.

My understanding of pickups was clear enough: the more, the louder; and you couldn't get much louder than Venom! Phil Collen from Def Leppard used a similar-looking guitar, with pickups filling all the space that they could. Well, this was sufficient to prove my point, wasn't it?

Of course not.

Whilst thumbing through *Kerrang!* a little later, I found a Van Halen feature. This was a result in itself: pictures, interviews, discussions about their music, etc. And then I found a picture of Eddie in full screaming shred mode. He was playing this strange-looking red, white and black striped guitar, and practically flaying it.

But it only had one pickup.

Now, come on, Eddie. What's the story with that?

Outwardly, he didn't appear to have mellowed. His guitar sound was still one of the heaviest around. But then, obviously, this was Eddie Van Halen. He was a magician, and he could play anything on anything! *Pas de problème!*

There was also the question of shape. This was fundamental and could be a particular issue with metal guitarists. Did you want to go down the conventional route of Fender Stratocaster and Gibson Les Paul, or were you into the more spiky, angry-looking gear such as the Jackson Randy Rhoads V or the B.C. Rich Warlock? Decisions, decisions... You didn't want to inadvertently go for something that looked a bit too mellow, you know, the kind of thing that Eric Clapton might have played. This could have had seriously negative cool implications, and it wouldn't really have sat all that well with trying to learn *Iron Man* by Black Sabbath. The Les Paul on the other hand? That was what Jimmy Page played, and there could be no doubts about Led Zeppelin's credentials. This was an interesting idea. But it was a little bit rounded, wasn't it? Not really all that aggressive-looking, and not really all that metal-looking either. Telecasters? Nah! On the other hand, anything with a V-shape to its body was absolutely fair game. Points and spikes, and lots of pickups of course. Instruments that could spear holes into partition walls. I'd seen guitars like that in magazines. Bands like Slayer, Megadeth, and the Scorpions played them. They were often photographed slinging them around, pointing their fretboards at the skies, and generally ripping shards of metallic music out of them. These guitars were, by definition, metal! The spikier the heavier and therefore the better. Simple, you see? It was clear that this was the kind of instrument I needed to be playing.

My research was done. It all seemed quite straightforward really. So I headed down to Derby's guitar shops to do a bit of browsing. There were a couple of shops in Derby at the time, and both looked well stocked. There was Foulds on Irongate and Carlsbro on Osmaston Road. Foulds was a really good place to look for guitars, but their focus seemed to be more on acoustic and classical instruments, and that wasn't the way I wanted to be heading. On the other hand, Carlsbro was hell bent for metal! There were stacked amps in the windows, long-hairs hanging about outside, and the prospect of serious hearing damage across the threshold. On walking in for the first time, I felt as though I had passed through some kind of portal into a different realm, where the guitars I had only ever seen slung over the shoulders of gods in *Kerrang!* were right there before me in the sizzling flesh. They seemed to have everything that a prospective metal shredder could ever desire. Guitars were hanging on the walls, floor to ceiling; guitars were in little islands in the middle of the shop floor; there were other guitars hidden at the back of the shop just out of view. In short, there were guitars flipping everywhere! Some of them even had skull pile and Grim Reaper graphics across their bodies! It didn't matter where I looked, there was always a guitar right in front of me. And then there were the amps. They were huge! I mean, some of them could have been used as castle ramparts, or as parts of an assault course. This was serious gear. What was it all going to sound like?

But there was one crucial consideration that I had failed to take into account.

Jeeesus Christ on a bike, this stuff was expensive! As I looked around, I realised that the price tags for the guitars were threaded in between the strings near the headstocks. *HOW* MUCH? Stone the bleeding crows! You cannot be serious!

It dawned on me right there and then that this was not going to be a cheap business. By no means. These things cost a bloody fortune! And I did not own a fortune. Far from it, in fact. Some of the guitars cost upwards of half a grand! I'd need to do a ram raid on Coutts Bank in order to raise that kind of cash!

And, of course, there were amps to factor into the equation. Obviously, you couldn't have an electric guitar and not have an amp. That would defeat the purpose. I took a tentative look at the Marshalls and winced. They cost about the same as the guitars! And naturally there were pedals and straps and leads and who knew what else…?

Rethink required. How was I going to get around this? I had pals at school who owned electric guitars and amps. And they were far from minted. They lived in very much the same way that I did with my family: comfortably enough, but far from being amongst the ranks of the loaded. So how did they get all these guitars? Had they borrowed them, been given them… nicked them…?

I was at a loss. I had to come up with a plan of some kind. I couldn't just drop the idea. That was not an option. I'd seen the promised land and I wanted a piece of it. But short of perpetrating some kind of smash-and-grab raid, I really couldn't see a way.

I moped about for a while. I was a teenage boy after all, and sometimes moping was just part of what I did. I believe that, occasionally, I was annoyingly good at it. A dubious quality maybe. But what was I going to do? I was a teenager with a serious case of acne, who wasn't all that interested in school, was a bit reclusive, and I had just found out that the barrier between myself and my dream of getting an electric guitar had gone up like the Berlin Wall: overnight!

But then it occurred to me.

The sky was clearly the limit in one direction, but what if I were to go the other way? That was a thought. Maybe if I went for the bottom of the barrel, I might come up with something through that route. A small chink of light appeared in the darkness. This was a possibility, and it could be a runner. I needed to visit Carlsbro again to see if they had anything which was, not to put too fine a point on it, cheap.

*

I visited again the following weekend. But this time I went with my eyes open, a little bit wiser, and with something realistic in mind. I did a bit of browsing, and inevitably a bit of awestruck gaping at some of the Flying V models, but what I really wanted to do was check out the bargain basement, maybe even the second-hand options. There appeared to be some guitars in the shop made by a company called Hohner, and they were on the slightly more affordable side, but they didn't quite cut it. Keep on going, Phil. There must be something here. How about this one? Squier. Wasn't that something to do with Fender? Could be. This looked like it might be a candidate. Three pickups, okay; black and white, all right then; tremolo bar, nice! And there seemed to be some kind of…

'All right there, mate? You interested in the Squier Bullet then?'

I honestly hadn't expected anyone from the shop to start *speaking* to me.

'Errrmm, yeesss,' I wheezed. The store assistant gave me a brief look. He seemed doubtful as to whether or not my balls had yet dropped. I was about fifteen, and fairly certain that they had.

'No problem. Come round the back and I'll plug you in. You need a pick?'

He confidently grabbed the guitar and led the way to the back of the shop.

I followed, as though in the wake of the Pied Piper of Hamlyn.

He took me into a small room in which there were huge amps and cables snaking around on the floor. There was a stool in the middle of the room, and he gestured for me to sit down on it. He then twanged out a few quick licks and nodded to confirm that all was well (in tune presumably). He plugged the guitar into one of the amps, rolled the volume up, and handed it to me.

'Right, mate, there you go. You're all set. Enjoy!'

He then left me to my own devices.

Christ almighty! I practically shat! I'd just been given, without even asking, my first shot on an electric guitar. And it was plugged into a Marshall in a soundproofed room!

I was caught completely on the hop, and I realised that I couldn't remember how to play anything. My head turned into a cavernous gaping vacuum. All those lessons I'd had with Mr Baxter, all that practising I'd been doing, all those Maiden tunes. Nothing. Nope. All gone. Jack Shit, your table is waiting! I fiddled with the knobs on the amp (I didn't know what any of them did) and then thought 'scales'. If I could play a scale, I could play a solo.

Theoretically.

The only one I knew was the pentatonic scale. That was the

one blues players used. It was also the one that Angus Young from AC/DC used all the time. I'd dabbled with that scale on my classical guitar, and basically knew where to put my fingers. But this was a different kind of axe. It was smaller, sleeker, and the neck was thinner. It felt totally unlike anything I was used to. And much, much better. This felt like rock! That was all well and good, but for the fact that my playing sounded like shite! Every time I even touched a string, the guitar buzzed and snarled and hissed angrily, as though defying me to play something at least half decent. I tried a few pull-offs and hammer-ons. I slid my left hand up and down the neck to get that *vroom* sound. I strummed a few chords. The noise I was making was messy, distorted, and it may have resembled music in some other universe, but in this one it sounded utterly shambolic. But it was great!

The door of the soundproofed room opened, and the guy from the shop poked his head in.

'Okay, mate? How are you getting on in there?'

'Amazing! This is fantastic! This is the best guitar I've ever played!'

I was clearly a bit more animated than I had been when he'd first spoken to me.

'Yeah, well, that one is pretty good to get started with. If you want it, it comes with an amp and a strap. It's yours for eighty quid. Not bad actually.'

Eighty quid? *Not* half a grand? And it came with an amp and a strap? It was a full set-up. Okay, it wasn't a spiky V-shape or anything remotely radical-looking, and it did, in fact, resemble the sort of thing Eric Clapton would have played. But that wasn't going to put me off.

Within a few weeks, and following a bit of negotiation with my parents, that axe set-up was mine. And this went further in confirming one simple fact: there is something inherently cool about electric guitars!

Accept	'Burning'
Black Sabbath	'Children of the Grave'
	'Sweet Leaf'
Def Leppard	'Bringing On the Heartbreak'
Iron Maiden	'22 Acacia Avenue'
	'Hallowed Be Thy Name'
Metallica	'For Whom the Bell Tolls'
	'Seek and Destroy'
Ozzy Osbourne	'Crazy Train'
	'Revelation (Mother Earth)'
Twisted Sister	'We're Not Gonna Take It'
Van Halen	'Ain't Talkin' 'Bout Love'
	'And the Cradle will Rock'
Venom	'In League with Satan'
	'Nightmare'

CHAPTER 6

'Holy shit, that looks nasty!'

As in every belief system, there are varying schools of thought. Some people lean in one direction, some in another, and some do their best to embrace all things.

Different strokes for different folks. Sounds reasonable enough.

Right back in the early days, when I was first getting my teeth into things metallic at school, I was up for whatever. If it was loud, guitar-based, and had big choruses and solos, then that was fine. All the boxes were ticked, and I was a happy camper. But all those compilations I had been listening to were serving to confirm something I had been suspecting for quite some time. The heavy stuff, and by that I mean the *really* heavy stuff, was hitting home. It was sinking in and becoming entrenched. Albums such as *Show No Mercy* by Slayer, *At War with Satan* by Venom, and *Kill 'Em All* by Metallica were hitting every single adrenalin switch in my body. I had to listen to those albums, and others like them, at full volume every single day. They gave me a huge shot of what I needed: a full-on musical head charge forced home with face-vaporising solos and raging thrash beats. Only albums imbued with this kind of unbridled aggression were able to give me that rush!

There was an attack in the music, and you had to work to keep with the pace, ferocity and complexity of it. And, if you could take it, you could build on it with further albums by the band in question or by seeking out others in a similar vein. It was as though the music was throwing down a molten gauntlet. Could you handle picking it up?

The other thing about this music was that it wasn't just a blizzard of guitars, drums, bass and howling vocals, it was genuinely technical and often extremely complex. Quite often whilst listening to thrash albums, I'd have to stop and rewind the cassette to check if I really had heard what I'd thought I'd heard. What was *that*? How the hell did he manage to wrench that sound out of a guitar? This happened quite a lot whilst listening to early Overkill albums. The intensity of the playing was insane! How in a million years was I going to be able to play like that? In short, this music was amazingly intricate, and the guys in these bands knew exactly what they were doing. On one occasion, quite naively, I decided to pick up my guitar and learn how to play 'Lucretia' by Megadeth.

Yep.

I know.

More fool me!

That track was an absolute wrist-breaker and, basically, I got nowhere with it. Even the intro was more complicated than most band's guitar solos. And the verse riffs were all over the place. I was one hundred per cent out of my depth, and scratching around on my fretboard wondering, 'How the hell am I supposed to even understand this?' How a bunch of guys could play something like that live, and pull it off note for note, was beyond me. I remember seeing Megadeth on stage and watching the two guitarists as they crashed through their respective riffs and solos thinking these guys were performing musical miracles right there in front of me! How was that music even feasible, let alone playable?

Over and above all of this, there were numerous other thrash bands out there, and they all started to crest the musical rise as the 1980s took hold. Anthrax, Heathen, Metal Church, and others stormed their way into my rapidly expanding cassette collection. It truly was an incredible time to be a thrash metal fan!

But then there was the other side of the coin.

The blatant contrast to thrash was a movement which was gaining ground and picking up speed at the same time. It had its clear origins in the 1970s with bands like the Sweet, Mud, and the New York Dolls, and, for the desperate want of a much better term, it became known as glam metal.

God almighty, I *hated* it!

Rarely in music have two sides of the same coin, which, at base, was essentially out of the same mint, been so different. Thrash and glam. Whatever one did seemed to be a blatant rejection of the other. They were at polar opposite extremes. The approach to music was totally different, as were the lyrics. And the image? Well, I'd started off with Maiden (a very good place to start), and from them I understood that metal involved long hair, T-shirts, tight jeans, cheesy grins, the occasional sweatband, and a load of stage gear.

Bases covered?

I had thought so.

But my preconceptions were about to be submarined.

The reason for this would have been all too clear to anyone looking at the Sunset Strip in Los Angeles during the 1980s. For metal bands in LA, it appeared to me that, first and foremost, and ostensibly putting all other considerations onto the back burner, the primary consideration was hairspray. And make-up caked on about an inch thick, featuring foundation, mascara, lipstick, and sometimes even a beauty spot.

Bloody hell!

We most certainly weren't in Kansas any more, Toto!

It happened one evening. It would have been a Friday, and

I was in a common room at Saint Hugh's. I was sitting there by myself waiting to be picked up for my weekend at home, and I was watching an old black and white TV set which had probably been in there for years on the basis of 'if it ain't broke, don't update it'. Fair enough I suppose. It worked well enough, but I did have to fiddle with a wonky coat-hanger aerial in order to get a steady picture. Having done so, I sat back and gawped at the screen. There was a music programme on, and it was just showing run of the mill stuff: background pop music. It was breezing by me and I wasn't paying all that much attention to it. Then, all of a sudden, the volume went right up, and guitars blasted out of the TV's tinny speakers. Heads up, Phil. Let's take a look at this.

There were four girls on stage playing rock 'n' roll, and playing it hard! They were slinging their instruments around like there was no tomorrow and the crowd was going wild for them. And, I've got to tell you, they looked damn good! They were wearing frilly blouses, very tight tights, and were made up to the nines. They were pouting, gyrating, and writhing on the stage floor. Ping! My adolescent antenna tuned right in. I leaned forward to get a better look at this bevvy of beauties. Okay, I could certainly enjoy this! And then the lead singer, the blonde with the really long hair, grabbed the mike and stared right into the camera's eye. Oooh yeah! This could be sweet!

But it wasn't quite what I'd anticipated.

Wow! Erm, eh? That's a husky voice for a lassie! And she's got a fairly squared off jawline too… And a suspiciously capacious-looking packet…

Hang on. Let me just try to reset my dials here for a second.

This looks like, just a sec… what's going on here?

Now when you bear in mind that I was a teenager who'd led a fairly sheltered life, and that I was away at school in what was actually a catholic seminary, things like this weren't really on my chart. As you can appreciate, sticking Iron Maiden and Black

Sabbath posters on the dormitory walls wasn't exactly smiled upon, but it happened anyway. Poison, however, was pushing things way further than I was able to absorb. This was top-shelf weird!

But Poison wasn't the first glam metal band I'd heard of. Not by a long shot. I'd seen pictures of Nikki Sixx and had heard bits of Mötley Crüe; I'd seen Twisted Sister albums in the shops; and I was aware of Hanoi Rocks. Even Ozzy Osbourne was going through a strange kind of post-lycanthrope glam phase at the time. But Poison was the first band of this kind that I'd ever seen in action, so to speak.

And it wasn't just the imagery of the glam bands themselves. If anything, they all seemed a bit soft to me. They wrote ballads and sentimental songs about being lonely and, shit, they used acoustic guitars! It appeared to me that they had completely missed the memo concerning what made metal what it should be. It was clear that these were the kind of bands which, at some point during their live sets, when they wanted to play a track 'for the ladies', were likely to say something torturous like: 'We're gonna slow things down a little bit now...'

Oh no you're fucking not, mate! That's not the way to play metal! *Aaaaargh!*

And then there were the names of the bands: I was seeing bands with names like Cinderella, Pretty Boy Floyd, and White Lion. Not really all that metal sounding, right? I mean, compare that alongside Nuclear Assault, Heathen, and Mortal Sin!

Additionally, and importantly, there was art. Now, I'm not talking about the type of thing you might find in the National Portrait Gallery or Tate Modern, or anything of that ilk. What I'm talking about is the most immediate indication of a band's likely 'direction': album covers.

Album covers were a dead giveaway. Thrash metal albums invariably had covers depicting something ominous or threatening. There was always a sinister feel as to what lay within the packaging of these albums, and I took this as an invitation. *Peace Sells... But Who's Buying?* by Megadeth is a good example. The cover art shows Vic Rattlehead (the band's mascot who crops up on most of their albums, just as Eddie does with Iron Maiden) standing in front of a devastated United Nations building. The sky is an orangey red, as though some pretty heavy incendiary ordinance had recently been deployed, and three fighter jets are shown approaching from the top left corner presumably to drop another clutch of bombs. Even the ground has been pulled up in slabs. Vic is facing the viewer and holding a 'For Sale' sign in his skeletal hand.

On first seeing that album cover, I remember thinking, 'Holy *shit*, that looks nasty! What the hell is *this* going to sound like?' There was no danger of encountering any teeny-bop treacle here! This album looked so metal you could be forgiven for thinking you would need to open the packaging with a blowtorch!

Then there was *Among the Living* by Anthrax. Its cover showed a strange, demonic-looking character, who had an uncanny resemblance to a certain TV evangelist, raising his hat and looking serenely on amidst a grid of subservient drones. And what about *Live Undead* by Slayer? This album was recorded live in New York in 1984, and the cover literally showed the band as a bunch of cadaverous zombies who had risen from the grave in some godforsaken cemetery to perform for their audience's delectation!

As a teenager with an increasingly lively interest in horror novels and all things supernatural, this kind of stuff not only hit the spot, it speared the bullseye and split the board! To prise open a record like *Live Undead* or *Haunting the Chapel* and smell the musical sulphur rising from it was incredible. What could a band that presented itself like that possibly sound like? Quite simple really: evil! That was what it looked like and that was what it sounded like. And that was what I was after. There were tracks with titles like 'Black Magic', 'The Antichrist' and 'Evil Has No Boundaries'. There was something here that was way beyond the pale. It was an invitation to shun the light and embrace darkness. I just dived right on in there!

The artwork was so important to me when choosing an album, even if it was by a brand-new or unknown band. There were always certain kinds of images on thrash album covers which reached out and said: *Try this band out; it's faster, heavier and more malevolent than anything you've heard before; think you can handle it?* It might have been the hooded monks for Testament's *Souls of Black*; it could have been Nuclear Assault's apocalyptic warning on the cover of *Survive*; or Onslaught's demonic imagery for *Power from Hell*. This was incredible stuff. It spoke to me in a way that the mainstream simply never could. There was something real and raw and unabashed about it. And the great thing was that the artwork was able to accurately anticipate the dark musical imaginations of the fans in question. It certainly had me hooked!

And, of course, there was Metallica. Their album *Master of Puppets* was, and still is, quite rightly, recognised as a classic of its kind. It was viewed with a type of reverence by young metal fans. This was a coming-of-age album. This was it! This was the one you had to own, and, damn it, you had to like it! Or else! I bought a copy on vinyl because with vinyl you were more likely to get a lyric sheet, and I needed to be able to follow the tracks word for word, riff for riff, and solo for solo all the way through. The back cover showed pictures of the band on stage in front of a huge audience, but what you noticed first was the front cover art. It was like nothing else any other band had ever produced. It showed rows of white gravestones standing in a grassy field. They were connected by strings to the hands which showed in the top corners of the sleeve, and this seemed to indicate that the fates of those interred had been predicated by masters of a higher power who could dispose of them at their convenience. On first glance, that was the totality of the image. In itself, it was instantaneously iconic. But then other more subtle aspects began to appear. I hadn't noticed, initially, that an American soldier's helmet was hanging from the side of the front left gravestone; or that there was a soldier's dog tag hanging delicately from the stone in the centre; and that there was an ominous-looking sunset glowing in the background. There was a solemn message within this image which suggested that this album was worldly, serious, and not to be taken lightly. There was a grim sense of reality about it.

But, underpinning all of this: MY GOD, THE MUSIC! There were only eight tracks on this album, but these were probably the best metal tracks I had ever listened to. There was so much light and shade all the way through them. There was the clean and sombre opening to the first track, 'Battery', which developed into an almost symphonic harmony section and then blasted into the most intense riffs, bridges and solos. Kirk Hammett blazed on this track! There was the middle section of the album's title track, which was one of the most delicately played and gentle guitar interludes I had ever heard. Then there was the relentless and ever accelerating jet-fighter thrash of 'Disposable Heroes'; Cliff Burton's genuinely extraordinary bass playing on the instrumental track, 'Orion'; and the near constant interplay between the guitarists throughout. No two ways about it, this was an extraordinary album, and it went beyond heavy metal, thrash metal or whatever kind of metal. This was verging on prog!

But the album I bought had a small defect. After I'd got it home and made sure that I had the living room to myself, I unveiled it and cued up side one on the record player. I then sat down with the lyric sheet to focus tightly on what was to follow. But something was wrong. It was nothing to do with the music. Where that was concerned, I was immediately spellbound. It was the lyrics. Nothing on the lyric sheet seemed to correspond with the track I was listening to. Uh oh! Had I inadvertently been slipped the wrong album at the shop? I lifted the needle off the record and took a look at it. Everything appeared to be okay. I turned the record over to try the other side. And then the light dawned. This was the right album. They had just put the stickers for side one's tracks on both sides of the record. Which could possibly make it a rare collectors' item now. But no, I'm not giving it away to anyone!

When I compared this alongside albums put out by glam bands, there were glaring differences, and I picked up on this right away. Whereas thrash bands predominantly used imagery of destruction, war, and sinister fantasy on their album sleeves, glam bands tended to use full-length pictures of themselves, usually in full stage make-up, and in pout mode. When I first saw the cover of Poison's debut album, *Look What the Cat Dragged In*, I briefly forgot that they were actually four blokes. Faster Pussycat's debut album cover was of a similar type but shot in black and white. I wasn't sure, but I thought the intention of the image was to convey a come-hither message to any willing ladies who might have been in their vicinity. Hmm... lucky them...

And, inevitably, there was Mötley Crüe. Throughout their career, the Crüe were well known for being about as subtle as a tight fart on a church pew, and you could always rely on them to max up the glam on their album covers. Their *Shout at the Devil* cover (after the initial pentagram sleeve had been banned and removed from stores) showed each band member glammed up to the ultimate max! They had their hair teased up, make-up slavered on like war paint, and they were wearing what looked like really heavy-duty bondage gear. This band meant business, and their business was pretty damned dirty. No doubt about that! If this had needed any clarification whatsoever, you only needed to look at the cover of their previous release, *Too Fast For Love*. This one featured a close-up, possibly cropped in, shot of Vince Neil's leather-clad crotch! Mötley Crüe were not interested in subtleties. No sir. If they could shove it in your face and slap you with it, then they were quite happy to do so!

Although a few thrash bands did indulge in make-up from

time to time, on the whole they didn't tend to bother with it. Long hair, jeans and some kind of vest which would allow the sweat to flow freely, were all that was really required. And the madder, the less posed, and the more psychopathic their appearance, the better. Overkill released an album in 1988 called *Under the Influence*. On the record's inner sleeve there was a shot of Bobby Gustafson, the guitarist, in full flow on stage somewhere. It honestly looked as though he was shaping up to eat the audience! He looked mad, wild and completely feral! That's what I'm talking about. They even opened the album with a track reassuringly entitled 'Shred'!

And that generally summed it up for me. Where glam bands were out there to look as pretty as possible, thrash bands certainly weren't thumbing through the Coco Chanel catalogue in search of *their* stage look. Their best pals in terms of aesthetics were probably odor-eaters and deodorants. They tended more towards the view of: 'Yeah! I'm ugly! Fuck you! Listen to *this* shit!'

Now there was an irony here, and it became clear to me at quite an early stage. I knew which side my bread was buttered on musically. But I was also a budding guitar player, and I knew good playing when I heard it, whatever its source may have been. I'd heard Kirk Hammett tearing through Metallica leads, and the amazing solos played by Alex Skolnick of Testament. On the other hand though, there was 'Eruption' by Van Halen sitting there at the back of my mind. That was still, by far and away, the most amazing piece of playing I had ever heard. But there was no way I could ever have seen Van Halen as anything other than a brilliant hard rock band. And, worryingly, there were also other incredible guitarists who were unquestionably of a more glamorous persuasion than I was aiming for: George Lynch, Warren De Martini, Kee Marcello, and others. Should a self-respecting teenage thrash metal fanatic really be into that kind of thing? I didn't want to look as though I'd gone soft. What would my fellow hairy thrash metal peers have thought if they'd found out that I was secretly glam-curious?

Anthrax	'Caught in a Mosh'
Bon Jovi	'Bad Medicine'
Cinderella	'Gypsy Road'
Europe	'Ready or Not'
Kreator	'Pleasure to Kill'
Lita Ford	'Kiss Me Deadly'
Megadeth	'Looking Down the Cross'
Metal Church	'Burial at Sea'
Metallica	'Ride the Lightning'
Mötley Crüe	'Shout at the Devil'
Poison	'Nothin' but a Good Time'
Skid Row	'Sweet Little Sister'
Slayer	'Angel of Death'
Tyketto	'Forever Young'
Vixen	'Edge of a Broken Heart'

CHAPTER 7

I was wide awake and bolt upright

I hammered my way across the school car park like I was being tailed by a wolfpack. I'd always been good at the hundred metres sprint, but there was a special urgency in this particular dash. It was Friday afternoon, and I had been selected to push the button that rang the bell ending the last class of the week. As I was careering on my way, I knew that the other kids, and probably most of the teachers, would be urging me to hurry the hell up so they could all clear off for their weekends at home. I scrambled through the arched doorway, up the stone steps, and along the corridor to where the bell button was situated. *BRRIIIIIINNNNNGG!* That's all folks! School is OUT!

Having done this, all I needed to do was wait for my parents to come and pick me up. I knew it would be a little while before they arrived, so I loitered around in the corridor and read some of the notices. As I was doing so, I heard a sound coming from the bursar's office, which was opposite where I was standing. Tap tap tap, murmur murmur, tap tap tap (scrape, bing), tap tap tap tap mumble mumble... Someone was dictating a letter. Well, whoopee-doo. Like I cared.

The following morning, back home in Derby, we were all having breakfast when the post arrived. Newspapers probably, and the usual takeaway menus. We sifted through it all and Dad opened a letter. He read it, looked up deep in thought, read it again, and then exclaimed: 'Bloody hell, they're closing Saint Hugh's!'

'*What?*'

'It's closing down. It says so right here. This is a letter from the headmaster, and it's dated, er, yesterday. It'll be shutting at the end of the spring term!'

'Why?'

'It doesn't really say why here, but, oh for fuc… for crying out loud!'

So, there you have it: school really *was* out. Completely!

*

Well, not quite completely.

Not as such.

There were, obviously, other schools to be found, and a few weeks later I became a pupil at the local comprehensive, which was a ten-minute walk from home.

It was not the most opportune moment for a switch of schools. A new exam system, GCSE, had just been introduced, and I was amongst the first kids to be subjected to this new and untested arrangement. Additionally, given that I'd had to switch school areas mid-year, I needed to catch up with a completely different syllabus. I was way behind right from day one. And above all that, most folk at this school, teachers and pupils alike, seemed a bit hazy regarding what was required of them. My English literature teacher even set a class essay entitled '*The Guinea Pig Year*'.

It was okay though. I found myself back with a lot of the friends I had had whilst at primary school. The classes were bigger and a lot noisier, and there were about thirty or so kids in most of them.

That was all right with me. In fact, I preferred it. At lunchtime, we played football instead of rugby; we didn't have to go to prep sessions when classes were over; and, something of a novelty for me what with having been at an all-boys school, there were *girls* everywhere. This was awesome, although, I've got to admit, I had absolutely no idea how they worked or what to do with them.

I had a couple of pals at this school, Chris and Ronnie, and we saw things in a similar light. We'd sometimes stay up in the classrooms during lunch breaks and listen to cassettes we had brought in. There was Cacophony and their album *Speed Metal Symphony*, which featured Marty Friedman and Jason Becker on guitar; there was the new Aerosmith album, *Pump*, which contained the single 'Love in an Elevator'; and, my favourite at the time, Kreator's *Extreme Aggression* album. German thrash. I couldn't get enough of it.

Then, one lunchtime, someone brought in a copy of an album which proved to be a bit of a mystery. It sounded like metal, but the guitar playing was so fast and complex that it ran away from you before you could get a proper grasp on it. All the songs were completely dominated by screaming and cascading solos, and the vocalist sounded like he'd had his balls jammed into an angle grinder. Wow, he could hit the high notes! This did not fit in with what we'd all become accustomed to. This turbocharged it.

What the hell was *this*? I gotta know!

And that was where I ran into one or two problems.

The guy who'd brought the cassette in wasn't all that clear about who the album was by, and there was nothing written on the side of it. All that any of us could be sure about was that the guitar playing was '*unbelievable*', '*incredible*', '*mind-blowing*', or just '*plain fuckin' sick!*' Understood. But what was this band called? I had no intention of being kept in the dark about this one. I asked the guy who had brought in the tape. Weirdly, he sounded a bit reticent about telling me.

'Well,' he said slightly hesitantly, 'it's by Wingy.'

'Wingy. *Wingy*?' I took a quick glance around the room to see if this registered with anyone else in there. Apparently not. I was met with a demonstration of shoulder shrugging and gobsmacked head shaking – don't ask us…

Had I heard him properly?

'Wingy? Is that the name of the band? It sounds more like… Come to think of it, I don't know what it sounds like.'

'Well, okay. Whingey… Something. Someone! Look, *I* don't know! It's this guitar player from Sweden!'

I could see that he was getting a bit agitated. 'Okay, okay, it's all right. I was only asking. I just need to know what this is. It's *amazing*! What's this track called?'

'Erm, I think it's called "Trilogy… Opus…" something.'

'What does that mean?'

'Look, *I don't know*! Jesus, will you just give me a break and *listen to it*?'

I decided that it was time for me to wind my neck back in and do what he said. I'm glad I did because shutting up gave me the chance to actually listen, which was, obviously, the whole point. Bloody! Hell! This was absolutely flipping off the scale extraordinary! There was some strange kind of alchemy going on here. The guitar playing was just explosive and constantly on the attack. This guy's playing went beyond what would normally be seen as metal. It was verging on classical.

After I had picked my jaw back up from where it had landed a few minutes earlier, and recovered the power of speech, I just said, 'Could you play that again? I can't believe what I just heard. Fuck me!'

I had to find out who this Swedish Whingey bloke was!

*

But, in the meantime, there was noise to be made. It turned out that Chris had an electric guitar and Ronnie had a bass, and they both had amps. Good start!

We decided that we needed to jam, and the music room seemed like the place to do it. There were amplifiers, cables and a lot of other paraphernalia in there. So we spoke to the music teacher, a Miss Crowe, to ask if we could use her room during some of the lunch breaks. I don't think she was very keen, and we had a feeling that she might not be. Let's say, she was known for being a bit testy. But, one way or another, we managed to prevail. Wide-eyed, innocent, butter wouldn't melt tactics probably.

But when we got in there the butter most definitely melted.

We turned the volume up so high we practically shook the walls! I, for one, had never been able to practise in a place with amps you could use on stage and turn them up to drum-drowning levels. It was fantastic!

We were, however, a bit limited in terms of what we could actually play. But we took a good stab at tracks like 'Am I Evil?' by Diamond Head, 'Fear His Name' by Overkill, and 'One' by Metallica. We could chug our way through the basic parts of these and at least make them sound recognisable.

How we sounded, Christ alone knows! I hadn't been playing all that long and didn't even use a pick at that point, just the nail on the back of my right index finger. And my guitar wasn't what you might call a metal tool. My Squier Bullet didn't realistically have the necessary cut and thrust for what I was attempting. But I thought that if I turned myself up loud enough, I could probably con my own eardrums. I suppose it sort of worked.

Beyond this, there was a further limitation: I couldn't play solos. This is a problem when you're a metal player. In metal terms, it should be viewed as a huge error of omission. By now, I was starting to get a bit more fluent with the pentatonic scale structure, but that was about it. If I knew which key we were playing in, then I could occasionally produce something half decent. But there were no guarantees. By way of self-improvement, I had bought copies of the guitar tab books for *Master of Puppets* and *…And Justice for All*. I had attempted, with mixed results, to learn some of Kirk Hammett's solos, and could make a scratchy attempt at playing some of them. So, on balance, I was better than some of the other kids at school. I reckon I could have been described as adequately crap!

Chris, who was a bit better than me, dealt with solo matters, whilst Ronnie boosted out root note bass lines at crunching volumes as he swung his mullet around. Ronnie also used to make Chris and me practically piss ourselves by doing scissor kick jumps off the desks whilst performing airborne Napalm Death grunts! He had that Lee Dorrian technique down to a tee.

But we needed more time to practise. There was no way we were going to perfect these tracks if we could only rehearse for an hour in school lunch breaks once a week. We needed to take these rehearsals away and jam at someone's house. We decided that Chris's place would be best. That was fine, but we lacked certain very important gear.

So, innocent little cherubs that we were, we nicked the school microphone.

*

There was a lot of tape trading going on at school. More and more of my pals were getting into metal. This was good, because it meant that I was getting to listen to what they were into just as much as I was lending out and making copies of albums I thought they should hear. One guy used to regularly come in with shopping bags full of copied cassettes and basically offer them around to anyone who was interested. He must have spent every waking moment cuing up albums for recording and writing out inlay cards. Good on him. That guy was committed to the cause. For every cassette he gave me, I did my best to give him one back. It was quite hard to keep up with him. His supply seemed endless. He was a pretty handy dealer, and never asked for anything in return. It was through him that I first heard *Painkiller* by Judas Priest. I'd never paid all that much attention to Priest before. I'd heard bits and bobs but ignored them for the most part. A short-haired bloke fronting a metal band? Seriously? Give me a break!

I didn't put the Priest cassette on as soon as I got home. This one could just simmer whilst I kept Metallica and Helloween on the boil. But one night I decided to put it on my Walkman after I had turned out the lights. I honestly wasn't expecting all that much, just basic, unremarkable, meat-and-potatoes metal.

But, oh how wrong could I be?

From the first hit of Scott Travis's colossal drum opening to the title track, I was wide awake and bolt upright. And I was rooted to the spot! This wasn't what I'd been expecting. It didn't sound like any other band I could think of. This was intense and electrified in the extreme, and the playing was as tight as a duck's chuffer! Whatever I had thought about Priest in the past, I took it back right there, lock, stock and barrel. This band from Brum was absolutely monumental! Every single track was stacked with drama, amazing lyrics, riffing that could blast your nuts into flour, and as for the guitar solos? – they were undeniably stratospheric. Glenn Tipton and KK Downing: they were both at the top of their game. Judas Priest had entered the 1990s with a sledgehammer of molten steel! How could I possibly have thought that I should overlook this album? It was completely indispensable! I went out and bought my own copy of *Painkiller* that weekend. What's more, I followed this up by going to see Priest on tour in March 1991. They played Sheffield City Hall and had Annihilator in support. And yes, they really were that good!

So, thanks very much to that guy for getting me into Judas Priest. I am indebted to you sir.

*

The school also had a common room for sixth formers. It was just a little room really, but there were a few chairs in there, a kettle, some posters on the walls, and a stereo with detachable speakers and a cassette deck. Granted, custody of the cassette deck was shared, so it could be L.A. Guns one day, the Smiths the next, and then Iron Maiden followed by U2. We played fair. But I evidently pushed the envelope a little too far when one day I proudly came in with a copy of Bathory's *Hammerheart*. A fellow pupil came into the room, heard a few bars of Quorthon's rasping vocals and crunching guitar, and the poor guy caved in. 'Fuck this shit!' He smashed his foot through the right-hand speaker!

And thus, our stereo departed this life in a shower of dust and a surprising amount of sparks!

*

It was shortly after this debacle that I ran into something I had never expected. A metal fan who was, in herself, a conscientious objector. She professed to be a fan of heavy metal, but she was completely opposed to listening to bands such as Iron Maiden, AC/DC, Metallica, or Slayer – namely, the best ones.

This made absolute zero sense to me.

It happened one afternoon just after a religious studies lesson. I had spent most of my time dozing my way through it, doodling in my exercise book and looking out of the window. After all, I seemed to have got the session pretty well sussed out: be nice to everybody, empathise whenever you can, and, err, well that's about it. I had thought that there might have been a bit more theological content to it than that, but if that was what was on the syllabus, then 'amen' to it.

As we were heading out of the classroom after the lesson, I

noticed that Carole was following me, matching me step for step. And she had started going on about AC/DC. She must have heard that I was a fan. She'd heard right. In any case, there wasn't anything wrong with that, was there?

Evidently, she begged to differ.

Carole manoeuvred me into a corner to ensure that she had my full attention. She looked semi-serious, semi-concerned, as though she had grave fears on her mind. She pointed her finger and looked straight at me. Then she began to lay it on thick:

'You do realise that the guys in that band are Devil worshippers. They're possessed. Their music is evil! You really shouldn't be listening to any of it.'

This sentiment lingered in the air for a brief moment as she stared at me, her eyes wide.

'Devil worshippers? What? You mean AC/DC are Satanists?'

She then shook her head and gave me an *are-you-really-such-a-vacant-moron* look. 'Of *course* they are! Haven't you listened to their lyrics? What do you think "Highway to Hell" is all about?'

To be honest, I had never really thought about the lyrics. My main interest was in the riffs, and I wasn't the most analytical of teenagers. 'It's just about driving fast and having a good time, isn't it?'

Carole responded with the supercilious treatment: 'Well, that's what you may think, but I know better. And you should too.'

Okay. Attempts to explain that members of AC/DC, and other bands about which she also proved to have serious apprehensions, probably spent more time in the pub than sacrificing goats to Lucifer fell on deaf ears.

'But, come on, Carole, you're a metal fan, aren't you? I thought you'd be right into that kind of thing. What about Testament and Megadeth? You've never listened to Slayer? You've never heard "Hell Awaits" or "Altar of Sacrifice"?'

Clearly not.

She then insisted quite steadfastly, and quite repeatedly, that she was committed to listening to Christian metal. From her point of view, only bands such as Stryper and Barren Cross were considered suitable. On the other hand, anything that sounded as though it might make any kind of reference to 'the dark side' was immediately dismissed out of hand. She was adamant about this, and the idea of listening to bands like Diamond Head, King Diamond, and Venom was completely out of the question. They were, in her opinion, harbingers of evil tidings. They had to be avoided at all costs or her soul would be in danger.

Carole gave me a doe-eyed look and whispered, 'Peace be with you.' Then she was gone.

Whether she was genuinely concerned or just being a pain in the arse was debatable. But I tend towards the latter. I wonder what she'd have said if I'd told her that one of my favourite albums at the time was *The Ultimate Sin* by Ozzy Osbourne.

Oh, and just in case it's preying on your mind, we did give that school microphone back.

Bathory	'Shores in Flames'
Helloween	'Phantoms of Death'
Judas Priest	'Hell Patrol'
King Diamond	'Eye of the Witch'
Kreator	'Some Pain Will Last'
Megadeth	'My Last Words'
	'The Conjuring'
Metal Church	'Watch the Children Pray'
Metallica	'Fade to Black'
Overkill	'The Years of Decay'
Ozzy Osbourne	'Killer of Giants'
Sammy Hagar	'When the Hammer Falls'
W.A.S.P.	'Heretic (The Lost Child)'
Yngwie Malmsteen	'Trilogy Suite Opus: 5'
	'Icarus' Dream Suit Opus: 4'

CHAPTER 8

Scant regard for life or limb

Clubbing.

For better or for worse, we've all been there. We've all experienced things that have made us cringe. Sometimes we have even been the subject of that cringing. We try to blot it out, but we know it's there. Like a guilty secret. Maybe time will erase these things from our memories and consciences; or maybe it won't.

Derby had its fair share of nightclubs, and they were much of a muchness. Most of them just played the same kind of music: trendy pop stuff taken directly from Radio 1, and standard 1970s disco tracks by the likes of the Bee Gees, the Jackson Five, and Gloria Gaynor. This sort of thing was okay in bits, but it was a struggle handling a whole night of it. Where were Led Zeppelin, Queen, and The Clash? What about the Stones and Thin Lizzy? Surely this kind of thing was just as applicable? If the DJs had put on 'Brown Sugar' or 'Another One Bites the Dust', I doubt it would have resulted in a mass evacuation of the club. But still, that's how it was.

Amongst others, there were clubs such as the Ritzy and Zanzibar, and there was also the decidedly dodgy Pink Coconut!

I went to the Ritzy once. I just want to underline that point: once. I wasn't so single-minded and set in my ways as to not occasionally entertain alternative approaches to life, and I did have quite a lot of friends of a trendier persuasion. And it was someone's birthday.

I had to put on a suit. I had to polish my shoes. In short, I had to make myself 'presentable' to a bouncer who would have the discretion to chuck me out before I'd even crossed the threshold. Much less than going for a night out, it felt more like I was preparing myself for a job interview!

I went, and I did my best to get into it.

But the truth dawned well ahead of the sunrise. I don't think I'd ever felt so completely out of place in my life. This was, most definitely, not my kind of haunt. There were mirrorballs on the ceiling; there were spinning disco lights; there were kids younger than me strutting around like they owned the place and trying to look 'hard' because they had a (probably watered-down) pint! There was not even the slightest suggestion of anything to do with rock music. Wrong, wrong! *All wrong!*

*

But there was one place which I fitted into perfectly, and I found out about it from a school friend of mine called Justin. Justin was also a big metal fan, although his leanings were more in line with L.A. Guns, Bon Jovi and KISS. Not really my flavour, but they were all different ingredients in the same big pot. That was what mattered. Rather than study, we used to spend most of our time messing about at the back of class, drawing hypothetical band logos onto the backs of our exercise books, and writing down lyrics and choruses for songs that we knew would never see the light of day. Whatever was being taught in class was largely secondary and that was reflected in our GCSE results. Let's just say, we weren't exactly star pupils.

One afternoon, I think during a geography class, Justin told me about a club called the Rockhouse. I hadn't heard of it, but he assured me that it was *the* place to be on a Saturday night if you were a metal fan in Derby.

Right. Received and understood.

And now, the details please:

Where is this place?

How much does it cost to get in?

What time does it open and close?

Will we need a taxi to get there?

The Rockhouse itself was a club on the edge of the city centre. It was a long upstairs premises above an electrical goods shop. Being another exercise in post-war red-brick facelessness, it wasn't exactly pretty to look at, but that would be to miss the point. It was what lay behind the seemingly uninviting façade that mattered.

Things usually got started at about 9.30pm, and there was always a long queue of leery-looking metalheads arrayed outside the entrance on Babbington Lane. By now, as I'm sure you can imagine, the 'dress code' was basically black gear, usually denim or leather, and a T-shirt, hopefully showing an album cover, from a carefully considered wardrobe collection. In direct contrast with other clubs that I could name, you were never likely to encounter any avuncular bouncers barring your way and saying: 'Sorry, mate, your T-shirt is inappropriate for this establishment. On your way now.'

The regulars were usually teenage schoolkids, like Justin and me, and a few more knowing and worldly folk in their twenties who looked as though they'd been around the block a couple of times. So there was always quite a lot of hair, quite a lot of zits, and a hell of a lot of black out there.

And then the dude with the key would come down the stairs of the club, pull open the door from the inside, and let us all pile in. Up one dark flight of stairs and turn to the left. You paid your entry at a little hatch and dropped off your jacket. Entry was two quid on the door – absolute bargain, by the way!

At this stage, the DJ would just be setting up his gear and sorting out what he was going to blast at the crowd that night, and the volume from the PA would be a little lower. The first stop would, naturally, be at the bar. There was quite a long bar area, and this was on the right-hand side of the main room as you walked in. It was well stocked. Additionally, drinks of choice were quite important back then, and they often denoted the musical preferences of the customers. It wasn't a hard and fast rule, but vodkas usually implied fans of the LA scene: bands like RATT, W.A.S.P. and Mötley Crüe. Jack Daniel's was unquestioningly taken by Guns N' Roses fans. After all, Slash appeared to live almost entirely on JD. Pints suggested fans of Maiden, Saxon, Priest and Sabbath. There was a certain taxonomy associated with customers' drinks selections, but, more often than not, this became a bit blurred after one or two rounds and it didn't take all that long before anything went.

As for the more elegant side of things such as wine and prosecco, I'm not sure if that even *existed* behind the bar at the Rockhouse. I certainly don't recall seeing any long-stemmed glasses in there.

Also, at around this time of the evening, the club would be just about smoke free. It was the only time that it would be though. One of the things about the people who went to the Rockhouse was that practically everyone smoked like Vesuvius. At that point in my life, I don't think I'd ever even touched a cigarette. But by about 11.00pm in the Rockhouse, you could be forgiven for thinking that you had wandered onto the set of *Sink the Bismarck!*

But who cared about that, because when the music started blasting, all other considerations dissolved into the background. Justin was right. It was amazing in there. It was as though the DJ had pilfered our music collections and was playing them back to us at volumes we certainly couldn't have got away with in our bedrooms. He detonated AC/DC, Deep Purple, Motörhead, Black

Sabbath, and the Scorpions into our eardrums. And he would not let up. It was relentless and absolutely bloody awesome! Track after track after track shot through and it fired me up like nothing else could. And, of course, there was no lightweight jigging about dancing going on. What you had at the Rockhouse was two lines of metalheads facing each other in front of the DJ area, as though having taken their partners. But rather than doing anything genteel, you essentially confronted your partner in an air guitar brandishing slam dive contest. It was basically a mosh-off! Hair was flying and fists were pumping all the way down the lines. And when you got a bit knackered, you just headed back to the bar to replenish your alcohol levels before diving back in again.

But what I looked forward to most was the 'thrash hour'. Maybe it was called that, or maybe it wasn't. I was never quite sure. By that point of the evening, it was just how my fairly pissed mind gathered together a long session of clearly thrash-based numbers. It was then that the DJ decided that the more mainstream stuff could take a break, and he would start hitting us with tracks by Metallica, Slayer, Exodus, Testament and Nuclear Assault. This was most definitely 'my bag'. I remember the very first track I got up for at the Rockhouse. It would certainly have been during the thrash hour. I just recall the DJ picking up the microphone and saying: 'You'll like this!' With that, he blasted out 'Whiplash' by Metallica! He was *damned right* I'd like it! I was up like a shot, and I leapt into that chaos with scant regard for life or limb!

After the thrash onslaught abated, the DJ would play some of the more commercial tracks of the day. 'Still of the Night' by Whitesnake was played every single Saturday night; as were 'Forever Young' by Tyketto, 'Sweet Child of Mine' by Guns N' Roses, '18 and Life' by Skid Row, and 'Blackout in the Red Room' by Love/Hate. 'Touch Too Much' by AC/DC and 'Bark at the Moon' by Ozzy Osbourne usually made it onto the playlist as well. Excellent!

And, naturally, you could make requests. If you had a particular itch for a particular track, you could go and have a word with the DJ. The odds were good that he would have it, and a few minutes later, after he'd made a few adjustments, it would roar out of the speakers. Of course, the DJ had to be able to hear what you were asking for, and at those volumes you had to practically bellow your requests at him. Sometimes it wasn't clear that he'd properly understood what you'd said, but the track you were after would usually be on his list in any case. So it didn't matter!

Also, I was one of those metal geeks. The type that are meticulous with their air guitar techniques. It didn't matter what was playing – it could be 'Fast as a Shark' by Accept or 'Under the Guillotine' by Kreator – I was always right on the money with the air guitar. I had every track down as though I'd written it myself, and the solos were all nailed. I never missed a note! I remember looking across the floor at the others out there who were clearly not aficionados of the AG and thinking, 'That's not how you play it, pal. Watch me. I've got these riffs sussed!'

There is a particular method attached to the proper application of the air guitar. The first thing to consider is that you actually need a surprising amount of space. If you're going to be swinging your arms around Pete Townshend-style, you need to try to avoid braining the guy standing next to you every time you belt out a power chord. Also, you need to consider balance. In order to play this instrument correctly, your feet should be positioned as far away from each other as possible, and you should be leaning in slightly towards your fretting hand. This is where the question of balance can become problematic, especially if this posture is coupled with quite a lot of head movement. Whilst accompanying thrash metal tracks, head movement is essential. If you were to inadvertently lose your centre of gravity, a number of things could happen. Firstly, you could go over backwards, crack your head on a table and knock beer all over a number of unsuspecting punters. Not good. Alternately, you could go over forwards, which would normally mean landing teeth first in another dude's trainers. On the other hand, if your inebriation levels were a little too high, you could just crumple down into yourself and end up as an unceremonious pile sprawling around like a dying fly. I've seen it happen. The fact is that there was always the danger of looking like a bit of a tool!

Been there, done that.

This was all well and good. How could a self-respecting metal fan find fault in a venue such as this? It delivered time and again. Well, as it happens, the Rockhouse did have an Achilles heel which everyone encountered at least a couple of times of a night. And that heel was the toilets. My God, the gents were minging, and even through the smoke, you could smell them well before you arrived at them. In the gents, there were two urinals and two actual closed-door bogs. And then there were the sinks… These were evidently just used as backup urinals for anyone who had overdone it a bit and simply couldn't handle the pressure of the long wait for blissful relief. Quite often, they were blocked up and brimming. Splashback was the least of your worries! Pretty gruesome…

As for the situation in the ladies' toilets, I can't say that I ever found out on a personal basis. I did hear stories about some chaps who occasionally got invited into the ladies for one reason or another (probably for a wee bit of 'how's your father?'), but they were usually pretty tight-lipped about their experiences in there.

I celebrated my twenty-first birthday at the Rockhouse. I was there with Andrew and Rob, and we went nuts that night. If I remember correctly (and I'll admit here and now that my memory of that night is a bit on the mushy side), we were shooting Jack Daniel's and slugging cans of Budweiser right from the get-go. Metallica had recently released 'Enter Sandman', and alongside that, metal was becoming bigger than ever. The music that night was right on form. Everything was fine until it came to leaving the club at the end of proceedings. For some reason we ended up going separate ways. Andrew and Rob apparently needed to get a taxi, whereas, following my liquid dinner, I had developed a craving for a postprandial kebab. So I headed off to McTurks, opposite the old bus station, to get a mixed doner with extra chilli sauce, and Rob and Andrew sidled off in the direction of a city centre cab rank.

What happened at the cab rank was never made absolutely clear. It seems as though a taxi pulled up, and Andrew and Rob stepped over to tell the driver where he needed to take them. Words were had, and Andrew told the taxi driver to 'fuck off!' This didn't go down especially well, until Rob, who was a bit flash with the cash at the time, produced a twenty-pound note and told the driver that he would tip him the change for what was effectively a fiver's trip. Well, money talked, and they probably got back home in about five minutes.

As for me? Not really sure. It was one of those blackout nights. I remember wandering off, handing over a fiver at the kebab establishment, and being given a pitta bread filled up with a huge splat of dubious-looking meat and sauce. I must have zigzagged my way back through the side streets whilst looking like a vagrant with a weird meat fetish. Not a pretty sight!

AC/DC	'Touch Too Much'
Black Sabbath	'Iron Man'
Extreme	'Get the Funk Out'
Guns N' Roses	'Sweet Child of Mine'
Iron Maiden	'Wrathchild'
Kreator	'Extreme Aggression'
Love/Hate	'Blackout in the Red Room'
Metallica	'One'
Ozzy Osbourne	'Bark at the Moon'
Sacred Reich	'Surf Nicaragua'
Skid Row	'18 and Life'
Slayer	'South of Heaven'
Van Halen	'Why Can't This Be Love?'
W.A.S.P.	'Animal (Fuck Like a Beast)'
Whitesnake	'Still of the Night'

CHAPTER 9

A slightly sore neck

When I was about seventeen years old, my band of choice was Sabbat.

Sabbat was a thrash metal band from Nottingham in the East Midlands. They had recently released their second album, *Dreamweaver*, and I had become practically obsessed with it. This band seemed to follow different rules to other bands of the genre, and this album made that all the clearer. It wasn't just track, followed by track, followed by track, until the end. This album actually told a story, and that was something I'd never run into with a metal album before. The story was set in medieval times and followed the journey of a young Christian missionary called Wat Brand on a quest to convert the pagans. What an amazing idea! It really got me! It was laden with mystical imagery, and with lyrics and music which practically transported you into the scenes. Just take a listen to the track 'Advent of Insanity'. Interesting...

Sabbat had been around for a few years and had been causing a stir in metal circles. Being local made them even more enticing. I was familiar with bands from Birmingham, London, and from further afield, but these guys were from just up the road. We were practically neighbours!

What's more, they were on tour and were going to be playing in Derby! What? No question. I was going. Anyone want to try standing in my way?

I'd seen numerous images of bands live on stage in magazines. I'd seen pictures of Slayer, Metallica, Def Leppard and others all going at it in front of thousands. I'd seen shots of the massive rows of Marshall stacks which seemed to be obligatory at metal shows, and of the crowds going mental. I'd seen pictures of guitarists playing Flying Vs, singers howling into microphones, and even drummers spinning upside down, but I'd never been in the crowd in front of these guys. I knew who a lot of the main players were: that Lemmy was practically a god in metal circles, and that Ozzy was essentially a massive hole you could pour beer into; but I'd never been closer to them than occasionally seeing them on TV or hearing them on my Walkman. But gigs appeared to happen somewhere just about every day of the year. I needed to get myself into the thick of the scene, and a Sabbat gig seemed like an excellent way to get started.

Sabbat's gig venue, the Darwin Suite, was a hall in Derby's Assembly Rooms. The Assembly Rooms itself was far from just a venue for gigs. Over the years it hosted all kinds of events, such as conferences, beer festivals, pantomimes and snooker tournaments. In fact, there was a time when national snooker tournaments, which often took place in Derby, were held and filmed there. Mum, Dad, Rob and I were all big snooker fans, so from time to time we'd head down to the Assembly Rooms to watch the boys on the baize. At this particular point, however, there was a poster plastered onto the box office window advertising a thrash metal show. I went into the box office and bought a ticket. I had committed myself to an initiation.

I had a few school pals who were interested in going with me. I might have had a few more if it had been INXS, U2, the Smiths or

A-ha that were playing. Where I was, metal fans were still viewed as an outsider bunch. You know, pleasant enough, but a little on the weird side. But such as it was, nothing was going to divert us.

*

We arrived early on gig night. It seemed like the sensible thing to do. There was quite a queue outside the venue, and we blended ourselves into it. Any passers-by on the square would have known there was a metal gig in the offing, even if they had been unaware of its scheduling and weren't even interested. A line of often spotty teenagers, all wearing black from head to foot, generally on the hairy side, and forming a fairly orderly queue outside the Assembly Rooms was always a telltale sign. We probably got some 'look at the *state* of that bunch of reprobates' and '*my* children would *never* be allowed to behave like *that*' looks and comments from the passing public, but we either didn't know or didn't care. We were heading to a metal gig, and our collective focus was sharp!

As was, and still is the case with gigs, arriving early does not necessarily compel the venue to open on time. As any hardened gig goers will appreciate, standing outside a venue which should have opened half an hour ago, occasionally in the summer rain or maybe in the winter sleet, is a frequent snag. Debutants such as I were unaware of this. As I understood it, 7.30pm meant just that; not quarter to eight. I'm sure I did a bit of watch tapping. Not to worry though. Stick with it and go with the flow.

Then, some forward shuffling and a few ironic cheers from the front of the queue indicated that the venue had opened. Right. Do the checks, as if I hadn't done them numerous times before I'd left home. Ticket, wallet, cash. And, of course, house keys, as I was pretty sure my folks would be in bed by the time I got back. All good. Excellent! The black line shuffled towards the door, and, as I got to it, a security guard checked my ticket. Without a second glance he ushered me inside. I followed the line up the stairs and into the venue proper.

There was music pouring out of a PA system somewhere, and then I saw, for the first time, a metal merchandise store. (I should point out right now that this was not my very first gig. I had been to see Fleetwood Mac and Pink Floyd with Andrew in 1988, so I was familiar with the implicit understanding that you definitely needed to *buy a T-shirt*.) There were T-shirts for both bands playing that night: the support band, Xentrix, who had come down from Preston; and Sabbat, who had presumably come down the A52. And there was also a curious smoky smell wafting around...

Having picked a Sabbat shirt – 'That one please, in medium' – I was kitted out and ready to rock. Or to do whatever it was you did at thrash gigs. Let's just say, I was in for a bit of an awakening!

In itself, the Darwin Suite was a pretty basic venue. On walking in, I could see that it was all standing, brightly lit, and about the proportions of a medium-sized club. Gig goers were milling around drinking beer, smoking, and chatting over the music from the PA. On stage there were endless ranks of Marshall amplifiers, and there was a kind of hum rising from them. The amps were divided at the back of the stage by a huge drum kit, which was set up on a riser. And above that there was a massive red and black spiky band logo backdrop: SABBAT. This was getting more and more real. I was, without doubt, exactly where I needed to be.

My pals and I placed ourselves front and centre, almost within reach of the stage. We wanted to get a good view, you see. After all, we were all avid Sabbat disciples, and we'd heard good things about Xentrix too. We wanted to be in the best place to absorb as much of this experience as possible.

As gig time approached, the music from the PA became louder, and some people in the audience started to get a little restless. A bunch of them were right up to the barrier now, and ready to get stuck right in. The volume of the crowd as a whole had risen with the volume of the music, and it was clear that something was about to be unleashed. There was an audible hissing sound as the smoke machine was switched on. Then, from backstage, the unbelievably loud crunch of an E chord blasted out. Flaming hell, it was loud! I looked at one of my pals, and he was clearly of the same mind. But his expression had switched from curious anticipation to *how-the-hell-do-I-get-out-of-here?* in that split second. He'd gone a funny colour. I looked back at the stage, and YEEAAAHHH! There they were! Xentrix! All four of them, clad in black from head to foot, looking a bit cocky, and, I thought, really cool with it. The guitars looked great. The lead singer, Chris Astley, was playing one which resembled James Hetfield's Metallica axe. Full marks for that!

He strolled up to the central microphone and got straight to the point: '*ALL RIGHT, YOU FUCKERS!*' The 'fuckers' in the audience were most definitely 'all right!' Collectively, the entire mass of people appeared to rise. And, right then, the band tore into a musical assault the likes of which my first-timer's mind had never imagined. As it began, the crowd crashed back onto the floor and, for a moment, I thought a huge fight had broken out! What in the name of *Christ* was going on? I was in the middle of an unbridled chaos of fists, feet, arms, legs, heads, and people literally being thrown across the top of the crowd! It was like being in the depths of Pandæmonium's most visceral cauldron! In short, I was getting the living daylights kicked out of me!

It was clear that I needed to rethink my situation. Getting a prime spot in front of the stage at a thrash metal gig was clearly neither the wisest nor safest thing to do. Unless you wanted to emerge at the end black and blue and potentially missing an eye or a tooth! I needed to get out of this riot. So, by fair means or foul, I barged my way to the back of the ruckus. Having escaped, I could see a bit more objectively what was going on. Essentially, the crowd of people, who until a few minutes ago had been sedately hanging around and having a few drinks, had gone collectively wild. I mean they were frenzied! And everyone seemed to be giving as much as they were getting. Beer was flying around, people's trainer-clad feet were sticking up vertically from within the surging melee, and there was a fair amount of sweat!

And the band on stage: well, they looked fantastic! They were pounding out metal, full throttle. The hair was flying, the solos were pouring out of the lead guitarist's fingers, and the drums were sounding like a Vickers machine gun! And the volume? Full blast! There was nothing subtle about a Xentrix gig. They tore through their debut album, *Shattered Existence*, and left many in the crowd, myself included, with jaws dropped and gaping.

Xentrix played for about forty-five minutes or so. I was transfixed. And I was also fairly knackered from the battering I had been taking. But this, as I was able to verify on numerous later occasions, was par for the course. I had just been inducted into the chaotic blood and guts world of the mosh pit!

Time for a pint and a bit of recuperation. My mates had completely disappeared. All trace of them had been obliterated in the chaos of the pit, so I headed to the bar by myself. It was crowded in there, so I had to wait for a little while. After a short spell, I got myself to the front and ordered a well-deserved beer. I had earned this through hard work and pure endeavour. Two large gulps and it was gone. This was thirsty work. My ears were ringing with a high-pitched 'eeeee' sound, and I was adrenalised to the hilt.

And we hadn't even got to the main event yet. This was just a warm-up; a bit of sparring before Sabbat came on to throw the real haymakers!

Everyone collectively drained their beers and convened (if that's the word) in the hall again. This time there was no casual standing around before things got underway. Everybody was pressing up towards the front of the stage, and some people were literally being forced back by security guards. There was an intense sense of aggression coming out of the crowd which appeared to be hardly containable.

The horde was now fully keyed up for the main event, and it was practically baying for blood! These guys looked prepared and ready to feed on raw kill! The lights went down, and the crowd rose again with a roar. And then the spoken, bell-chiming, crow-cawing intro to the *Dreamweaver* album played out through the PA. There was a brief, but loaded, silence. Then… *Christ almighty!* Hell broke loose! The lights came on, and the black-clad long-haired band tore into their first track with unbelievable speed and tightness. The energy and the singularity of purpose coming from the band was clear to see: they wanted to create outright mayhem in the crowd. They succeeded. The mass of people in the pit practically exploded! And what's more, I had got into the swing of it now. The mosh pit no longer held any fear for me. I was hurtling around with the best of them. Pushing, shoving, barging, charging. I felt like a seasoned veteran!

I was right in front of Sabbat's guitarist, Andy Sneap, and was absolutely fascinated by the way he dug the metal out of his Fernandez Flying V. His blond hair, which reached down to his waist, was flying as he clobbered the riffs through the Marshalls. It was technical and fast, but it looked effortless as he shredded out the solos. There were, naturally, solos in every track.

Martin Walkyier, the lead vocalist, was constantly right at the front of the stage, and he had a crazed, possessed look in his eyes! His stage gear was absolutely considered with this sentiment in mind. He wasn't just wearing a loose-fitting T-shirt, or anything like that, he was up there in full-on battle gear, leather-clad and sword wielding! He was inciting the crowd to get more and more fired up and was locking eyes with people as he did so. He was dripping with sweat after the first track.

Being a fan, I knew all of the tracks from their albums, word for word and riff for riff. But there was one track in particular that I was hoping they would play: 'I for an Eye' from their debut album. Lyrically, it was a kind of dialogue between God and Satan in the context of Milton's *Paradise Lost*. I was in luck. Partway through the gig they blasted this one out. And I think that was when it started. There was nothing else for it: I decided that I needed the full immersion experience. I wasn't the type to merely stand around and watch, passively, when people were jettisoning themselves around left, right and centre. Not my style, pal. I needed some of that action! I hoisted myself up onto someone's shoulders and threw myself forward onto whoever was in front of me. I then sort of swam over the tops of numerous bodies until I got to the stage. Having clambered onto it, I stood up and got myself right to the back where the Marshall amps were stacked. I could see the back of Fraser Craske as he pummelled his bass. For a brief moment, I thought, 'Holy bloody crap! Fuck me! *I'm on stage with the band! AAAARRRGGHH!*' I went for it. A direct sprinting charge past Sneap and Walkyier and straight at the crowd in front of me. At full stretch, I threw myself headlong into the swirling mass! This was it! This was so real, and so absolutely metal!

Sabbat's set was longer than Xentrix's, what with them being the headliners. They played for about an hour and a quarter, and finished off with their anti-evangelical showstopper, 'The Church Bizarre'. By the end, I was knocked about, bruised, sweat-drenched, and high as a kite! This seemed to be the same for everyone else there too. I don't know if I'd ever seen so many huge smiles on the faces of so many like-minded people ever before in my life. There was a real feeling of community and allegiance amongst us. It was like being part of a tribe and standing in absolute accord with the other members, even if it was my first metal gig. Admittedly, I had been a bit naive at the start, and this had resulted in the brutal extraction of seven shades of shit, but by the end I was fully up to speed and match-fit for whatever metal music could throw my way.

That night had been one of those 'eureka' moments: I had most definitely found what I had been looking for!

As I walked home afterwards, my head was still racing. I got back in about half the time it took me to get out to the Assembly Rooms in the first place. I threaded my way back through the streets and passed the Seven Stars pub, a listed building with a superb jukebox. (It was a biker bar at the time, you see?) I let myself back in, and my parents were actually still up and sitting in the living room. I shudder to think what I must have looked like. A sack of shit tied in the middle was my guess! My folks didn't seem to mind. They were just really pleased that I'd had a good time. I was, and still am, grateful for this.

I was riding the adrenalin for several days after the Sabbat gig and remember telling some of my less metal disposed friends at school about it. I'm not sure if any of them really knew what I was blethering on about, but it didn't bother me. I had a spring in my step, and a slightly sore neck.

*

Just one more thing…

I was studying at Mackworth Tertiary College in Derby a couple of years later, when I saw an advert for guitar lessons pinned to a noticeboard. I took a closer look, as a bit of tutoring could never do any harm. Suddenly my eyes locked and I stared at it, stunned: 'FORMER SABBAT GUITARIST AVAILABLE FOR MUSIC LESSONS. CALL NEIL WATSON ON THIS NUMBER.' I stood rigid for a few moments reading the advert over and over again. Was this serious? Could I be just one phone call away from getting lessons from Neil Watson? I'd seen him playing on Sabbat's Berlin concert video which had recently been released, and he was clearly a really solid player. I was feeling a bit starstruck. Should I call him? What should I say if he picked up the phone?

I called him; and he picked up.

He asked me what I was into, what kind of gear I had, and how long I had been playing. I gave him a brief rundown of what was what, and he told me to come on over for a trial lesson.

I went over the following week and started a course of the best guitar lessons I had ever had. I mean, this guy could play! And what's more, he was interested in the kind of thing that I wanted to pick up on, namely, metal. He showed me soloing techniques, scales and picking styles. He was also really chuffed that I mainly wanted to learn Sabbat stuff. He showed me the riffs for 'The Clerical Conspiracy', 'Do Dark Horses Dream of Nightmares?' and 'I for an Eye'. At one stage, he pointed out that he was glad I wasn't asking him to teach me 'Surfing with the Alien' by Joe Satriani, because he had no idea how to play that one!

Guns N' Roses	'Out Ta Get Me'
	'Paradise City'
Iron Maiden	'Can I Play With Madness'
	'Moonchild'
Megadeth	'502'
	'In My Darkest Hour'
Metallica	'Eye of the Beholder'
	'The Call of Ktulu'
Sabbat	'Horned is the Hunter'
	'I For an Eye'
	'Mythistory'
Sodom	'Agent Orange'
	'Remember the Fallen'
Xentrix	'Balance of Power'
	'Crimes'

CHAPTER 10

The power of thrash compelled me!

Maybe concerns about teenage boys and guitars and the likely implications regarding homework are well founded. The year 1990 seemed to confirm this. Understood: I knew that a bit of work would be required in order to pass A level exams. As it happens, I only did a bit, and that turned out to be the wrong bit, because I failed spectacularly. In two of these exams, I didn't even get a grade.

Bollocks!

Oh well, so much for that. But there again, I wasn't overly bothered because I wasn't all that interested in studying in the first place. A levels just appeared to be the correct and logical next step for a sixteen-year-old who had a handful of GCSEs. And what had been my subjects? Religious education, English literature and geography. Now there's a spurious combination if ever I saw one! I clearly had no conventional ambitions where the workplace was concerned.

I wonder if any of you have ever been in this situation. You're seventeen and at school, and you have been told that the careers advisor will be coming in next week. You have been asked to do some sort of research into likely workplace scenarios for your future, and to consider possible options such as medicine, the law, teaching, accountancy, yada, yada, yada...! You are in the position, in short, of not having a fucking clue what some of these things even *mean*, and yet it has been recommended that you consider one or other of these loosely defined paths to take as your destined route through life up until the age of sixty. Familiar?

I was one of those kids whom the careers advisors hated. It wasn't because I was offensive to them, or that I spent my time picking my nose or cutting farts during our sessions. It's simply because I was that kid who didn't care about employment ambitions on their terms. I had my guitar, and that was to be the tool of my trade. You could say that I was already in training. This, however, cut no ice with my interlocutor.

After the customary handshakes and 'hello' pleasantries, she would ask me if I had any specific ambitions regarding my future. I would explain to her, again, as the same advisor came repeatedly to our school, that my ambition was to play lead guitar in a band.

The conversation would then degenerate into something along the lines of what follows:

'Hmm, yes, well that's very interesting, Philip, but I don't think I can recommend anything like that.'

'But it's a job, isn't it? I thought that was the point. And I think I could be really good at it!'

Well, yeeeessss... But it isn't what I'd recommend. You see, what you need is an occupation with a career path which will give you satisfaction and security for the future. Have you ever considered accountancy?'

'Nope.'

'What about the law? Now that's an option I often discuss with people your age.'

'The law? Like going to court and things like that?' (yawn...)

'Basically, in a way, sort of, yes.'

Does that mean joining the police?' (scratch...)

'Well... possibly...'

'...Nope.' (streeetch...)

At this point my mind would usually get a bit foggy and I'd start to drift. I would begin thinking along the lines of: 'I wonder how Eddie Van Halen got that guitar sound at the start of 'Atomic Punk'; or, what would Metallica sound like if they still had Dave Mustaine in their ranks? or, Lita Ford: Mmmm...'

I would be brought back down to earth by the careers advisor realising that she was fighting not only a losing battle but a pretty much pointless one at that, and saying that it was about time we wrapped things up for this session.

That was always fine with me, and we'd go through the customary 'goodbye' pleasantries. That would be it for the next six months.

I don't think she liked me very much. She never seemed to do very much smiling during our meetings. Or maybe she was just like that with everyone. I don't know. Either way, she wasn't interested in *my* career ambitions at all. I had hoped for a bit of encouragement rather than 'no, no, no' followed by head shaking and a reproving waggy finger. I was just honest. I knew what I wanted to do and that was it. A private one-to-one consultation in a classroom served no purpose as far as I was concerned. Waste of time.

That said, shortly after I left school, I got a job temping at the Crown Prosecution Service in Derby. It was just photocopying and filing, menial things like that, but I did get to follow the odd solicitor to court from time to time. Maybe I had gone into law after all.

*

But that was all secondary to me. Academic, you might say.

Heavy metal was thriving!

The year 1990 was an amazing one for metal music. The scene went nuts! It hit the hyperdrive button and burst full blast into lightspeed! The end of the 1980s had been incredible. Take 1989, for example. Overkill released *The Years of Decay*, which I thought was even better than their *Under the Influence* album. Metal Church's *Blessing in Disguise* and Testament's amazing *Practice What You Preach* albums both came out. Also, if you factored in *The Headless Children* by W.A.S.P. and *Trash* by Alice Cooper, you had what could be described as a damn good year for the headbanger!

But then 1990 happened and a perfect storm of mayhem was unleashed! Megadeth released *Rust in Peace*; Slayer released *Seasons in the Abyss*; Anthrax released *Persistence of Time*; and Gamma Ray, which had formed around Kai Hansen, who had removed himself from a rapidly disintegrating Helloween, put out the extraordinarily upbeat, optimistic and, dare I say it, happy, *Heading for Tomorrow*. On top of this, AC/DC produced *The Razors Edge*, which featured the immortal track 'Thunderstruck'; Extreme released *Pornograffitti*; and Steve Vai had a massive hit with *Passion and Warfare*. And of course, whilst all of this was going on, Guns N' Roses was rapidly becoming a juggernaut. The scene was leaving metal fans staggered. How much better could this get?

It was clear where *my* money was going to get spent!

In every edition of *Kerrang!* there were reviews of new albums by the hugest bands on the scene, and they were all coming out with the KKKKK recommendation. I had a subscription to that magazine now. I didn't even need to go out and buy it. It just dropped through the door with the regular mail. Stuff reading the *Daily Telegraph. Kerrang!* had the only news I was interested in keeping up with!

*

And then the tour of all tours was announced. I saw the poster advertising it in Way Ahead Records, and I had to stop, rub my eyes, and look again. This couldn't be, could it? No, give me a break. You're dreaming, mate.

But let's take another look, just in case…

The bands' jagged logos were screaming out of the artwork, and they demanded compliance.

What? Suicidal Tendencies, Testament, Megadeth, and Slayer? On the *same* bill? On the *same* stage? On the *same* night? *THE CLASH OF THE TITANS!*

Ho-lee-shit Batman!

Sometimes your hand gets forced. This was one of those occasions. I knew damn well that tickets for this show would disappear like shit off a shovel! So I had to get in there, and I had to be quick! Missing out on this was not worth even contemplating.

The power of thrash compelled me!

*

There was a distinct buzz about this gig. People whom I didn't even know were metal fans were dashing out to buy tickets, and a pretty decent contingent of us piled into various parents' cars for lifts down to the Birmingham NEC on the night.

We arrived at the arena, found the entrance we needed, and headed on in. We were met by a number of substantial security guards who didn't look especially interested in the night's proceedings. But there again, they had a job to do and it was no real hassle. A quick frisk, a pat and a slap, and that was about it. 'No, officer, I am not carrying a concealed weapon.'

The merchandise store was loaded with interesting goods. But what to choose? With so many alluring options on offer, the discerning punter would need to think carefully. I wasn't a massive fan of Suicidal Tendencies at the time, so maybe I would rule out their gear. Testament? Nice shirts, but I was only in a position to buy one. So, what was on offer from the Megadeth and Slayer 1990 autumn collections? Firstly Slayer. Now this was a striking one. Naturally, it was black. First things first. And on the front was an image of all four band members' heads on spikes! Right. Okay. I hadn't quite expected that. Some kind of pentagram imagery perhaps, but not multiple decapitations! Then I heard someone pipe up behind me: 'Ah, they're just copying what W.A.S.P. did on their *Final Command* tour. Only thing is, *they* had *their* heads spiked up on the stage! I hope they cleared it with Blackie!'

So onwards to Megadeth. This was an interesting one, and it fitted nicely with the *Rust in Peace* album cover imagery. The print showed Vic Rattlehead, their long-time album cover mascot, in some kind of military high command control room. Behind him was a digital map of the world showing multiple missile trajectory routes. Vic had his skeletal finger poised over a red button with 'LAUNCH' emblazoned above it. Money changed hands, and I changed shirts. It's always nice to get new clothes.

We had seats up on the side of the arena looking down at the stage from the left. We were fairly close to the front and quite high up. It was a good spot. Right down at the barrier would have been better, but up here was just fine. No complaints whatsoever. Thousands of people were pouring in, and we could see them gathering in the floor area and hanging around by the merchandise store. We could also see across to the seating on the opposite side and at the back. The place was filling up with more metal fans than I'd ever seen together in one place. This truly was a major event. And it wasn't just a one-off – the Clash of the Titans was a tour, and the NEC was just one venue along its route. This monster was going to prowl across much of Europe and the USA.

Metal music was pumping out of the house speakers and, as we waited, the growing crowd was clearly starting to get more and more wired up. Roadies were scuttling around on the stage making sure everything was ready to blast. They were checking the microphones and shining torches around. Still more and more people were filling up the seats and the pit in front of the stage. I was up there in my seat, my eyes nailed to the stage, thinking come on, come on, come on, let's get going! Let's break the seal on this! *COME ON!*

And then, all of a sudden, they did. Suicidal Tendencies burst onto the stage and started cranking out their *Lights... Camera... Revolution!* album. And my God, they were going for it! Prior to that, I hadn't been much of a fan; they were a bit on the funky side for my liking. Seeing them live changed everything! Wow, they were tight, and the tracks all made more sense now that I was seeing them being played right there in front of me. The sound technicians in the NEC had got it just right: everything, even at those volumes, was as clear as a bell. The band burst through what was, admittedly, quite a short set, but they clearly made a point: they were not a band to be messed with. Mike Muir was stomping left and right across the stage as though he owned it, and Rocky George was shredding like a lunatic. They were on the Clash of the Titans bill with good reason. What an opener!

Suicidal Tendencies finished to a roaring ovation, and after a very short interval Testament stormed the stage. Now this was old-school thrash. In fact, Testament was one of the first thrash bands I had ever heard. They had just released their *Souls of Black* album, and they ran through a blazing set which incorporated several tracks from it, and a lot of their earlier material. Chuck Billy was right up front as usual brandishing his mike stand like a warrior would his spear. The guitar playing, as you can imagine with the likes of Alex Skolnick and Eric Peterson on stage, was blistering! This was a band on form, and the crowd knew it. All around us there was hair whipping back and forth, and contorted-faced fans who were bellowing the lyrics back at the band. Air guitars were being slung left, right and centre. And this was just in the seats. In the pit in front of the stage, a serious mosh situation was rapidly developing.

Again, it was a fairly short set, which lasted about an album's length. But it was intense, focused and brilliantly delivered. This gig was hotting up, and it occurred to me that this was not just a gathering of bands and fans; this was a major event in musical history. Some of the best exponents of metal were showing just how good they could be, and they were going down a storm.

And next we were going to get Megadethed! They were touring their *Rust in Peace* album, which was recognised as a classic almost as soon as it was released. How could it not be, with tracks like 'Hanger 18', 'Tornado of Souls' and 'Five Magics'? And with Marty Friedman playing lead and Nick Menza on drums, this was a line-up which saw them at their peak. The crowd was practically blowing a gasket now, and when the house lights went down and the huge album cover banner lit up across the entire back of the stage, it roared like a massive pack of rabid lions! Then the spotlights came on and whipped across the crowd, dragging their glowing beams chaotically around the arena, whilst a Mustaine-voiced public service warning announced the declaration of martial law, curfews, and death penalty consequences to the non-compliant! This was a band that clearly meant business, and as the members came onto the stage one by one, the crowd went fanatical.

And they hadn't even played a note yet!

Dave Mustaine pressed 'Launch'!

They kicked off with 'Rattlehead' from their first album. Perfect! This couldn't have been a better opener, and it set the tone for a show which would be unremittingly intense. Their playing really was as good as it was rumoured to be, and Friedman and Mustaine's riffing and soloing was clinically precise. How could a band be that tight when the music they were playing was so fast and technical? They nailed every number. They snarled their way through 'Wake Up Dead', 'The Conjuring' and 'Devil's Island', but for me the high point, if it was possible to pick out one particular instance during this set, was 'In My Darkest Hour', in which Mustaine shouldered his double-necked black Flying V and played what can only be described as one of the keystone metal tracks of all time!

I was practically beside myself. I was screaming, bellowing and screeching out every single lyric like some kind of possessed harpy! And this seemed to go for everyone else in the crowd as well. Megadeth knew how to lay a thick seam of insanity through an audience, and everyone in the Birmingham NEC had been drawn right into a whirlpool of focused craziness. It was incredible!

And then they finished their set with their cover version of 'Anarchy in the UK' by the Sex Pistols! I couldn't believe it! Relentless to the last! This band was like a huge demonic muscle that just kept flexing and flexing and flexing, and they left the crowd genuinely amazed.

I turned to my pals, and they turned to me. We didn't say anything. We couldn't. There were no words to adequately describe what we had just witnessed. Megadeth had played for just over an hour and had laid waste to the NEC. We all knew that we had been participants in something that had been authentically fantastic, and we just stood in front of our seats with frozen-in-time expressions.

And, of course, it wasn't over yet. Not by a long shot. Slayer had yet to come on. They were also already viewed as a legendary band. Their *Reign in Blood* album put that beyond any dispute. But they were now two albums further into their career and they were building and building on that foundation. Slayer's most recent album, *Seasons in the Abyss*, had been a huge seller amongst metal fans, and they were known for their extremely aggressive delivery on stage. This was likely to be a bruising performance!

Once again, the lights went down, and the massive crowd roared in response. All around there were screams of *SLLAAAYYYERR! SLLAAAYYYERR! FUCKIN'... SLLAAAAYYYYERR!* I was starting to get a bit hoarse by this point. After hollering out the lyrics to every track in Megadeth's set, it was hardly surprising. But you soldier on, don't you? I wasn't going to let a touch of laryngitis hold me back. And I *loved* Slayer! I'd been jamming along to Slayer tracks for years now, and I loved the way Jeff Hanneman and Kerry King put riffs together. Their style seemed to tune into the dark part of my musical psyche perfectly. I continued to throttle my vocal cords and howled on with the baying masses.

Suddenly, in the pitch darkness, we heard a huge crash of thunder rumble out of the PA system. This was followed by the sound of a torrential downpour. We were then hit by Dave Lombardo's unmistakeable triple blast on the drums. You've got to be joking! They were going to start their set with a showstopper! 'Raining Blood'. *AAAARRRGH!*

And then the band was on, and they blazed with both barrels. When a band starts off at 100mph and then ups the pace, you know you're in for an experience which will remain in your memory. Slayer did just that! If anything, they were even louder than Megadeth. Tom Araya's whiplash-inducing headbanging style was on full display, and his voice was in screamingly good form. The riffs, the harmonies and the power chords shrieked through the arena, and the lights were kept low and a deep red. We were experiencing something infernal after all.

They ran through a set of classic tracks, both old and new, and were actually shockingly good. They played 'Black Magic', 'Die by the Sword', 'Spirit in Black', and a favourite of mine which I had been willing them to play as soon as I had heard about the gig: the vampire-inspired 'At Dawn They Sleep'. I could feel the double bass drums thrumming through my thorax, rattling me to the very core! As Slayer played, the lighting rigs above the stage lit up in the form of immense inverted crosses, both left and right, sending out their beams to the farthest reaches of the arena.

For all his bellowing, Tom Araya came across as a genuinely

pleasant dude. Between tracks he chatted with the audience, asked people to keep an eye on each other in case somebody in the pit got a little too pulped, and generally played the very genial host. Following these interludes, he would scream out something like '*WAAARRRR ENSEMMBBLLEE!*' at which point the craziness resumed with a raging vengeance!

Slayer ended their set with two further showstoppers: 'South of Heaven' followed by 'Angel of Death'.

By the end of the night, when the house lights came back on, I was physically and mentally ragged. And my throat was wrecked. And all of this took place on Saturday 13th October 1990, the day before my nineteenth birthday. This had been an incredible way to usher in a new year!

And by way of a wee extra pressie to myself, I grabbed a half-priced Slayer T-shirt from a guy hanging around outside the venue. Probably dodgy, but a good deal is a good deal!

AC/DC	'Moneytalks'
	'Thunderstruck'
Anthrax	'In My World'
	'Intro to Reality – Belly of the Beast'
Gamma Ray	'Lust for Life'
	'The Silence'
Jon Bon Jovi	'Blaze of Glory'
Kreator	'People of the Lie'
	'When the Sun Burns Red'
Megadeth	'Hanger 18'
	'Tornado of Souls'
Ozzy Osbourne (Randy Rhoads Tribute)	'Believer'
	'Mr Crowley'
Slayer	'At Dawn They Sleep'
	'Live Undead'

1984. *Plugged in and absorbing everything. Presumably listening to Iron Maiden.*

You start off with air guitar, and then you graduate onto this!

Rob's not a guitar player. But he

At school with my first ever electric guitar. I'm ready to rock.

In Huddersfield with a white B.C. Rich Warlock. I may have had a few beers…

Rob joined the army after leaving school. Here he is in Kenya.

The Palace of Culture and Science in Warsaw.

Andrew, Rob and me drinking beer somewhere in Germany.

Iain performing with SKY9 at Ivory Blacks in Glasgow.

*John playing
bass with SKY9
at Ivory Blacks.*

Paul behind the kit at Ivory Blacks.

Me hitting a G chord at Maggie Mays in Glasgow.

Santie with Tribal, an Appaloosa mare whom she used to ride in South Africa.

Mum and Dad at our wedding.

With Mr Richard Parker, my best man. He's also an awesome guitarist.

With my bride.
What an amazing day!

Sound check before
the reception.

Just some of the gigs
I've been to...

CHAPTER 11

It was like that scene in Hellraiser...

'*God almighty!* What the hell's *going on* in there? It sounds like someone's *throwing up!*'

Dad had stuck his head around my bedroom door just as I'd hit play on side one of Pestilence's *Testimony of the Ancients* cassette. Now, from a personal standpoint, I would view that album as a classic of its kind, but opinions in the household varied.

In short, I was on my own.

It's safe to say that my family, as a whole, wasn't especially enamoured with my choice of death metal as a musical preference. Whatever could have been the matter?

Could it have been down to the relentless speed and shrapnel-like ferocity of the music?

Nothing wrong with that, was there? I'd have thought my folks would have been sufficiently accustomed to that kind of thing by now.

Was it something to do with the low tuning of the instruments, and the way this layered the distortion of the metal even more thickly?

Problem?

Maybe it was something to do with the guttural vocal style.

Well, yes. Perhaps they had a point on that score. All things considered, '*UUUUURRRRGGHHH!*' doesn't imply a great deal of melodic content. Rob was distinctly not into it. Whilst I was playing death metal albums, he would sometimes come into my room red-faced, with his hands over his mouth and his cheeks puffed out. Then, using authentic straight-from-the-diaphragm sounds, he would simulate barfing his guts up!

But none of these diversionary tactics were going to push me off track. The more extreme this music was, the more fanatical I became about it.

*

A couple of years earlier, rumours had started floating around in the metal press concerning an extreme scene in the USA. Just about everyone who was interested in metal music had been aware of these rumours. The word on the street was that, somewhere in Florida, a snarling beast was on the rise, and that it was now reaching out around the world with bloodied claws which were intended to lacerate eardrums and senses.

There were album cover images appearing in the metal magazines of the time, and they were seriously different to what I had seen before. They reminded me of the artwork for Death's *Scream Bloody Gore* album, but somehow these were on the more malevolent side. There was an underlying feeling of stygian menace in these images. And they kept on appearing again and again. Then the bands' names had started to crop up: Morbid Angel, Deicide, Sepultura, and Nocturnus to name but a few. It wasn't clear at the time what kind of sonic assault would be levelled at me by bands like these, but I had a feeling that this would be a listening experience like no other.

But the term 'death metal' was nothing new. I had heard it used with reference to thrash bands like Slayer. This label suited them nicely. The principle subject matter of Slayer's lyrics were Satan, war and death. That was all broadly applicable.

But this was something else, something clearly much darker, and it was emerging with great speed and a voracious appetite.

So, naturally, I had to dive in, and I jumped right into the maelstrom.

The first death metal album I bought was *Altars of Madness* by Morbid Angel. It was their debut, and it was released in 1989. I wasn't sure what kind of buzz I would get from this, but I was pretty single-minded, even though a lot of fellow metalheads at school had told me, 'You can't buy an album by a band with the word "angel" in their name! They'll be crap!'

Diversionary tactics? See above...

I headed down to Way Ahead and picked out the CD from the rack. The album art for *Altars of Madness* was bizarre in the extreme. It showed a twisted mass of fanged ghoulish faces staring out at the viewer. When I flipped the CD over, I was presented with pictures of the band live in concert. *Fucking hell!* Their regular gig could have been to the cave trolls in the Mines of Moria! I mean, these guys looked out-and-out demented! Especially the lead vocalist/bass player, Dave Vincent.

One of the guitarists, the curiously named Trey Azagthoth, was shown playing a B.C. Rich Ironbird guitar – one of the most aggressive-looking instruments ever devised. It was a jagged spikey red affair, and it could mean only one thing: that this band went all the way over the top. There were no limits or compromises to be had here. Nothing subtle could come out of an instrument shaped like that!

Beyond all of this, there were the titles of the tracks. I'd like to think that by this time I had been initiated into most things metal, and that my mind was fairly broad. By now, I had been listening to the likes of Iron Maiden, Megadeth, Slayer, Kreator, and many others for some time, and titles such as 'Wrathchild', 'Devil's Island', 'Ghosts of War', and 'Betrayer' were bread and butter stuff to me.

However, on running through the track listing on *Altars of Madness*, I could see that I was entering a different kind of territory altogether. It was like that scene in *Hellraiser*, when the wall in Kirsty's hospital room splits open and she walks into a section of the Cenobites' maze – and runs into The Engineer... There was something genuinely sinister going on here. The album started off with 'Immortal Rites', and then, amongst others, track titles were 'Lord of all Fevers and Plague', 'Bleed for the Devil', and 'Suffocation'.

What exactly was I getting into here? Motörhead, Saxon and AC/DC all appeared quite conservative by comparison. Their tracks tended to be about historical events, motorbikes, or, sometimes, just plain humping. Morbid Angel on the other hand appeared to have been released directly from Hell with a mission to bring its diabolical message to the world. There was also a suggestion that Trey Azagthoth ritualistically cut his right arm prior to gigs so that the blood would pour down onto his guitar as he played! Was this guy actually for real? Well, as it turned out, he was!

The entrance to a shadowy abyss in my mind gaped open. Yup. Whatever this was, I had to have a piece of it. This absolutely suited my need to reach for the extremes. I'd experienced thrash and loved it, and that wasn't likely to change, but Morbid Angel were clearly primed to add an even more intense level to the sound. I knew that this wouldn't be everyone's cup of tea, but it certainly proved to be my blackened poison chalice!

I picked up the CD and headed off to the cash desk. The chap behind the counter raised his eyebrows and nodded in a kind of *you're going for it* gesture.

In short: they delivered!

I got back home and holed up in my bedroom. I put the CD

into the player, pressed play, and braced myself. *Bloody hell!* What was going on? Track one began, and I couldn't quite work out what was happening to start with. This album came with a side order of vertigo! The intro to the track ripped out of the speakers, and it sounded as though the music was trying to tear itself apart! It was contorted and twisted. Had this been recorded backwards? I froze for a second, genuinely perplexed. Then Pete Sandoval smashed out a gunshot snare drum hit. A bludgeoning riff kicked in. And then the vocals began.

Up until this point, metal vocal styles as I had understood them were usually shrill, high-pitched, fast, and sometimes even bordering on operatic. Given that much of my reference came from Iron Maiden, Helloween and King Diamond, that was entirely understandable. But with Morbid Angel things were a bit different. Here the depths were being plumbed, and the cavernous guttural swell which rose from Dave Vincent's larynx came hotfoot from Hades!

I had honestly never heard anything like *this* before. It was a ferocious and ruthless assault. There was uninhibited violence unleashed on this album. Sandoval went beyond even the limits of Dave Lombardo of Slayer, or Ventor of Kreator. The drumming was so unbelievably fast, and yet it was completely under control and tight with everything else.

The guitar solos were frantic, chaotic, and often apparently formless attacks on the whammy bar. God knows how Trey and Richard Brunelle were able to keep those guitars in tune! Or maybe the guy downstairs knew better, and he was aiding and abetting in their endeavours.

There was also the issue of the lyrics. They seemed to be ritualistic, and they also appeared to be authentic in the way they were expressed. Whilst some bands were a bit tongue in cheek with their lyrics, Morbid Angel were fully committed to every malediction they expressed. They referenced demons, profane and blasphemous practices, and hallucinatory visions of ancient arcane gods. This band was wholeheartedly committed to darkness. In fact, to underline this, a few years later they recorded a track entitled *Sworn to the Black*.

I was hypnotised. I was mesmerised. I was possessed!

As far as I could see, my quest for extremity was complete. This was a full-blooded rampage. I loved it!

Take me down to the infernal city!

*

Then I had a stroke of luck. As I mentioned earlier, I was seriously into collecting heavy metal compilation albums and regularly used them as a way of fleshing out my collection. I was in Our Price Records in Derby one weekend, just having a browse, when a cassette cover caught my eye. This was a new one. The album art showed a gated entrance to some kind of spectral subterranean realm. The gate had creaked open, inviting the viewer to enter and commune with the creatures that lurked within. I picked it off the shelf to take a closer look. The sky in the picture was an orange-red: a storm was about to break. On either side of the gate sat demonic creatures beckoning the curious observer. Interesting and alluring. After all, intense and dark imagery is fundamental to the metal experience. The title of the album I held in my hands was *At Death's Door: A Collection of Brutal Death Metal*. I flipped the cassette over and found that there were twelve tracks on it, many of them by bands I had never heard of. It featured bands such as Morgoth, Cerebral Fix, and Exhorder. More extremity. More forbidden fruit. There was no way I could leave the shop without it.

Sold!

*

Sepultura's 'Mass Hypnosis' kicked things off. These four guys from Brazil lashed out amazingly and set the pace for what was to follow. They certainly picked up a fan right there and then. It wasn't long before their back catalogue found its way home with me.

There were some fantastic genre-defining tracks on this album, but the one which struck me hardest was by Deicide. I had most certainly heard of *them!* Within the metal community there were few that hadn't. This was largely because, irrespective of any musical standpoint, these four guys from Tampa, Florida were generally viewed as frankly unhinged. The rumours surrounding them suggested that they were active, enthusiastic and practising Satanists. It had also been suggested that their lead vocalist, Glen Benton, was so far gone in this direction that he had branded his own forehead with an inverted cross. This turned out to be more than just a rumour. Any footage of Deicide either on stage or in interviews clearly shows the cross imprinted on his forehead even to this day. The picture of the band on the cassette card was a little worrying as well. What exactly was I seeing? The members of Deicide were glowering out at the viewer, and their faces were completely red! And I don't mean that it just looked as though they had been holding their breaths for a while; I mean absolutely blood red! It looked more like they had been let loose in an abattoir and told, 'pick your cleavers'!

This was seriously messed up, no doubt about it! Whether it was blood for real or just a doctored photograph set up to generate as much controversy as possible, I couldn't say. For all I knew, it could have been food dye. Either way, this was far out stuff.

First impressions, eh?

Beyond this, there had been protests by religious groups and others outside venues where they'd been scheduled to play, and there had even been bomb scares at shows!

So, when I got to Deicide's track 'Dead by Dawn', I wasn't sure what I was going to be dealing with. Was this just going to be a more intense version of Slayer or Venom? Were they just rehashing

Iron Maiden's *Number of the beast*? Was it all just a gimmick? Or was this something entirely new which reached beyond its predecessors?

Ladies and gentlemen, boys and girls: welcome to Hell!

You were given no warning. They cut straight to the chase. Steve Asheim's drumming was the fastest I had ever heard, and the guitar solo at the beginning of the track built up in a swell before exploding like a nail bomb! And the guitar riffing was an engine of out-and-out devastation! When Glen Benton's vocals began, the insanity of this band made itself completely apparent. They weren't vocals. They went *beyond* vocals, and even H. P. Lovecraft may have been inclined to raise an eyebrow. There was definitely something very weird happening, and I sat looking at my stereo speakers thinking, 'What the fuck is actually going on here?' Embedded within the vocals there was a kind of tortured howling and growling. It sounded like something was trying to get out and its plan was to throttle the listener and drag them down into the netherworld! I thought there might have been a fault with the tape. I took it out and checked it hadn't got tangled in the player. Nope, all appeared to be normal, at least on the surface. I put it back in again and hit play. Abnormal service resumed and the insanity carried on and, if anything, got more and more intense. The rasping, gasping and snarling continued. And then, just as abruptly as it had begun, it was over. I hit stop on the cassette player. I had to. There are certain things that give you reason to take a quick breather. A violent initiation into the world of Deicide is unquestionably one of them.

I will suggest something though: if you've never listened to any death metal before, or even if it's just not really your thing, try listening to 'Dead by Dawn' by Deicide one night after you've turned out the light. I dare you. Consider the nightmares you'll have to be a bonus. Chances are you'll be having them for a while. Of course, it is possible that your neighbours might get in touch with a local exorcist...

Some of the tracks on *At Death's Door* hit so hard that I had to play them over and over again. So, I think that at this juncture a few honourable mentions would be appropriate. Firstly, the track 'Culte des Mortes' by Cerebral Fix, who were a band from Birmingham. The pounding drums and guitars on this track, and the flat-out moshiness which accompanied them, damn nearly put me in a neck brace! I spent hours and hours jamming to this track, and the way the mood of the track changes for the outro still blows me away. There was also 'Last Abide' by Sadus, a band from California. The frantic vocals and Steve Di Giorgio's unique bass playing style really made this track stand out.

There was no question about it. Death metal had me firmly in its grasp, and I was quite happy to let its grip tighten. Also, so many bands were emerging at the time that I was spoiled for choice. Even the more mainstream record shops started to market these bands. Fair enough, they weren't pasting album covers all over their windows and walls, but if you took the time to look, you might have been able to find some interesting gems in these outlets. The first time I encountered the New York band Immolation was when I saw a CD of their debut album *Dawn of Possession* in the rock/metal section of a branch of the HMV shop in Derby.

That said, as the subtitle of the *At Death's Door* album indicated, *some music was meant to remain underground,* and a lot of these bands and their albums never saw the light of day in the more regular market. They were just too far out. Also, a lot of the album art was so radical and intensely nightmarish that shelving it alongside Stock, Aitken and Waterman stuff like Kylie Minogue, Rick Astley and Sonia would probably have been a little too incongruous. I couldn't envision the managing directors of the HMV shop giving the green light to putting a twelve-inch sleeve of Cannibal Corpse's *Eaten Back to Life* album in a rack right alongside *Ten Good Reasons* by Jason Donovan! No...

But, of course, I knew which shop I needed to visit when I wanted a shot of this kind of stuff!

*

Then came Christmas. We were all there: Mum, Dad, Andrew, Rob and me. We did all the usual things: drank too much, ate too many chocolates, pulled crackers, and enjoyed Mum's amazingly good roast turkey lunch. Nobody I know can even come close to making gravy like she does! It was a full family get-together, in the best of traditions.

Now I wonder what could have been in my letter to Santa for 25th December 1990? What could a metal music fanatic, such as I, have requested from the guy who drops pressies down chimneys?

A skateboard? No.

A Scalextric? Not this year.

The newly released and uncut edition of Steven King's *The Stand*? Hmm... well maybe...

Cliff Richard's latest carol, 'Saviour's Day'? Far from it! Nose held and chain pulled on that one!

As I clawed away the wrapping paper from a thin and suspiciously flat foot-wide square which was in my present pile, I unveiled the blackened cover of Deicide's self-titled debut album. Just the band logo in the top left-hand corner to begin with, and then the full front cover showing the occult symbol, which apparently represented some demon or other. I remember my dad saying, 'Oh wow! You've got a record. Let's have a look!' He took a look at it, turned it over, gave me a slightly doubtful glance, and handed it back.

'Erm... Merry Christmas, Phil. Enjoy!'

Cerebral Fix	'Culte des Mortes'
Death	'Evil Dead'
	'Spiritual Healing'
Deicide	'Deicide'
	'Sacrificial Suicide'
Entombed	'Left Hand Path'
Malevolent Creation	'Premature Burial'
Morbid Angel	'Immortal Rites'
	'Visions from the Dark Side'
Nocturnus	'Andromeda Strain'
	'Lake of Fire'
Possessed	'Seven Churches'
	'The Exorcist'
Sepultura	'Mass Hypnosis'
	'Troops of Doom'

CHAPTER 12

It's a wild world in there

Death metal was the pinnacle. Music couldn't get any darker or more extreme than this. And the more vicious and over the top, the better. A lot of thrash bands and other metal bands were, naturally, indispensable. I mean, what would life be without Megadeth, Maiden and Motörhead? But death metal opened up a different world: something more forbidden, something murkier, something tangibly sinister. The mainstream was simply not cutting it in the same way. For me, it was all about blast beats, growling, grunting, snarling vocals, and lyrics about Satanism and just about every kind of evisceration under the sun.

Ahh, bliss…

Death metal had a relentless brutality which rammed all my lunatic dials right up to the red lines. There was nothing else like it. And it was more than just escapism: you could get that through watching *Bill and Ted*, *Back to the Future* or *The Lost Boys*. This was more to do with plumbing the depths of your own imagination and using the music to stir up its dark contents.

The Deicide and Morbid Angel debuts were enough to get me started. They *were* classics then; they *remain* classics now. I used to play those albums in my portable CD player at volumes which were verging on unbearable, and I absorbed every lyric, every time change, and every slam diving solo.

*

A brief note on personal development…

Paint a mental portrait of this: a studded belt, preferably leather if affordable; black jeans; hair which was, in all honesty, a damn disgrace; the blackest T-shirts with the most menacing imagery I could dredge up; huge trainers; and still, annoyingly, quite a lot of zits! I was also a bit surly in those days, and death metal seemed to complement this nicely. On top of that, my reading habits had headed down a seriously dark pathway. Dabbling in Edgar Allan Poe was one thing; some of his stories and poems are unbelievable.[2] I was also getting heavily into books about real-life hauntings, possession and exorcism. I had started to collect an ever-growing library of this kind of thing. Books by David St Clair, and accounts of cases dealt with by Ed and Lorrain Warren were becoming regular bedtime reading material.

I also tried reading some books by Aleister Crowley, but, to be frank, most of them sounded like completely incomprehensible bollocks!

So maybe I was one of the odd kids. Very probably. Genial, but strange… But still, I knew what I was into, and I went for it hell for leather!

*

Morbid Angel were becoming big news in the extreme music scene. With the controversy they had generated, and their first album,

---

2   If you haven't read any of Poe's stories, I recommend getting stuck right in. Start off with 'The Pit and the Pendulum'. Wow, that's gruesome stuff!

which was a real game changer, this made good, good sense. There were full page features on them in *Kerrang!* with photographs, interviews, and gig reviews. The live shots looked incredible. The band showed a real ferocity on stage and an uncompromising commitment to delivering the most hostile shows possible.

And they were releasing *a new album*. The previews had said it was going to be called *Blessed are the Sick*, and that it was likely to be a bit more experimental than their debut. That was fine with me. These guys could experiment in any way they chose. I was ready for anything!

And they were *going on tour*. Even better, they were scheduled to play at Rock City in Nottingham. That was just one city away from where I lived.

And, oh my God, they were doing a *meet-and-greet signing session* at the Nottingham branch of Way Ahead on the afternoon before the gig!

Well, what's a death metal fan to do?

Straight to the box office to book my slot! This gig was going to be a fast seller for sure. And there I was, next day, ticket in hand. MORBID ANGEL: THE WORLD SICKNESS TOUR 1991, NOTTINGHAM ROCK CITY, 15 MAY.

This was going to be massive!

Sadus were playing the support slot. I'd never heard any of their albums, so I did the right thing and searched them out. It turned out that they had released an album called *Swallowed in Black* in 1990. There was homework to be done. I needed to buy this album and study it before gig day. Which I did. They played a totally different style to Morbid Angel. One of the first things I noticed was Steve Di Giorgio's amazingly intense bass. I'd first heard this on their track 'Last Abide', which had featured on the *At Death's Door* compilation. His bass seemed to weave and meander and tangle its way through every track. The guitar soloing was frantic but perfectly put together. And then there were the vocals. Again, totally different. It wasn't your usual low guttural death metal style. Darren Travis reminded me of Mille Petrozza of Kreator. And that was to his credit.

On the day of the gig, I kitted myself out in the blackest gear I could find, which included my black denim jacket. I was justifiably proud of this jacket, and it demonstrated that I had earned my stripes as a metal fan. The back of it was pretty much plastered with patches. There was a huge Overkill patch dominating the top. I'd picked this up at a gig they'd played at the Astoria in London during their *Years of Decay* tour in 1990. And beneath it there were patches for Slayer, Megadeth, W.A.S.P., Dark Angel, and others. I was hoping to find a Morbid Angel patch in the merchandise store at Rock City.

The band was doing the meet-and-greet at about 2pm, and I joined a huge line of black T-shirt wearing devotees which stretched away from the door of Way Ahead. There could be quite a long wait before I got to the front of the line. The new album had been released a week or so earlier, and it had certainly fulfilled its promise. But I hadn't brought my copy with me for fear of it getting pulverised during the show. However, lots of folk said that they were going to get their tickets or jackets signed instead. Good idea. Why not? A signature was a signature, it didn't matter what it was on. As the line shuffled forward, we got the usual *Oh God, look at the state of that pile of wreckage* looks from some of the passers-by. Not a problem. You develop an immunity to it after a while.

Onwards, onwards, shuffle, shuffle. Fortunately, it wasn't raining. There were the usual discussions within the queue, and they normally started off with a remark about a T-shirt and the tour dates printed on the back. Where had you seen such and such a band? When was that? On which tour? Was it at a festival? Also, as we were primarily discussing death metal, the answer to the 'What were they like in concert?' questions were quite consistent: 'They were fucking *brutal*, mate!' Nuff said.

Closer, closer, and then I was in. The place was rammed. I had joined quite a long queue, so fair enough. The mood music was blasting out at a higher volume than usual. There were Morbid Angel, Obituary, Deicide, Bolt Thrower and Sepultura shirts being worn everywhere. You could barely move for black T-shirts, denim, leather, hair and huge boots.

I scanned the faces in the shop... *Hey, that's them!* Well, two of them at least. Maybe the others had headed out for a slash. They were human beings and may have been in some of Nottingham's pubs over lunchtime. That would have been understandable. There were, and still are, a lot of good watering holes in Nottingham.

There was Dave Vincent propping up the cash desk, pen in hand, actually looking quite a lot shorter than I had imagined. He was signing tickets and shirts and jackets and bags. Whatever came to hand really. I realised I'd better get my ticket out quick. This was my moment. I needed to be cool, collected and prepared when I passed it to him for signing.

All of a sudden, it was my turn. And guess what? I fucked it up!

'All right, mate? Err, how's it going?'

I must have come across as barely verbal, let alone interestingly articulate.

He gave me a *you're-definitely-a-first-timer* grin, whilst probably thinking, 'Holy Belial, what the hell am I dealing with here?'

I proffered my ticket, and he scrawled his signature on it. He then looked me in the eye and gave me a vice grip handshake. Okay, good job. Now move on.

Standing next to him, tall and gangly with a big toothy smile and hair absolutely everywhere, was Mr Trey Azagthoth. The lead guitarist. The one with the red B.C. Rich Ironbird. I was a bit more prepared this time. He stuck his hand out for shaking, and I shook it. 'Give me that ticket, man! I'll sign it for ya!'

'Cheers, Trey. Love your red guitar, man. Coolest axe in metal!'

'Cheers, *maaan!* You may be seeing it tonight! See ya!'

And then I was away, and back into the normal reality of the shop feeling a wee bit starstruck. I had just *met* Morbid Angel. Well, half of them. But still, it was bloody *fantastic!* And now I was so fired up for this gig!

*

Rock City was jam-packed that night. It must have been sold out. And the merchandise stand was loaded with all kinds of goodies and memorabilia. Predictably, I went for a T-shirt. The print showed a skeletal figure who appeared to be playing some kind of bone as if it were a flute. It had a caption beneath: *Leading the Rats.* It was the grimmest, most metal-looking shirt there; and, in fact, the grimmest, most metal-looking shirt I had ever seen! Tour dates on the back? Check. No argument. Sold. And a patch too. A small square one. That would fit in nicely.

I was ready to get into that mosh pit and let it rip!

I'd learned a lot since my blooding at the Sabbat gig in Derby. I was braced for a bruising and ready to deal one out as well if necessary. After all, being in the pit is as much about the music as it is about plain survival. You put yourself in harm's way out of choice, and you have to be able to handle yourself. It's a wild world in there!

I barged my way right up to the barrier for Sadus and found myself standing a few feet away from Steve Di Giorgio. Now, this man could play bass! I'd never seen anyone play bass like that ever before in my life. He was like the death metal equivalent of John Entwistle. His fingers were flying all over the neck of his fretless instrument, and he never needed to check what he was doing!

Darren Travis dominated the middle of the stage and howled his way through the set. This band was so tight, even at the speed they were all playing, and the double bass drumming hammered out through the midst of it all. They blasted through 'The Wake' and

'In Your Face', and were, in the words of the guy I had overheard in the queue outside Way Ahead, fucking brutal! I had to grip the barrier so as not to get clattered off it by the raging circle pit that had churned up behind me. And it was hot in there. Sweaty, dripping, piping hot! I needed a drink, and I needed it right away. But the bar was way behind me, and I didn't want to lose my place. I'd found the prime spot in front of the stage. If I split, there was no way I'd be able to get back to the barrier through that crashing morass of humanity which had erupted in Rock City.

So I stayed put and stuck it out. It's what you had to do at gigs like that. There was no room for compromise, and personal wellbeing sometimes had to take second place. You had to roll with the punches. Sadus played for about forty-five minutes, and they were ruthless. What an amazing support band. And on top of that, at the end of their set, miracle of miracles, Travis appeared to have some spare four-packs of lager on stage. He split the packs and handed the cans out to the fans up at the front. That was the perfect thing to do at the perfect time. They were chugged and drained in moments. As much as anything else that happened at that gig, I remember those lagers. Hats off to you, Mr Travis, you're the man!

The switchover from band to band was pretty quick. Rock City was always good for that. In some venues you had to wait and wait and wait for the headlining band to come on after the support had finished, with endless roadies tapping the mikes and going 'two two, two two' into them. Not so at Rock City. They just liked to get right on with things.

And next, Morbid Angel. What were these guys going to be like? Their new album had shown a major development in their songwriting. Some of the tracks from *Blessed are the Sick* had taken a very different approach. Rather than being played mainly at breakneck speed with blast beats and screaming guitar solos, many of the new tracks were much slower, and consequently heavier with it. They were like huge creatures, lumbering and thundering their way across scorched and barren landscapes. These tracks made an impression and left a mark. In short, they were amazingly written and devastatingly heavy. And it was clear from the outset: they'd recorded *another* classic.

Then the lights went down, and the audience was plunged into pitch darkness. The sizzling feedback from the new album's opening track fired up through the PA. Needless to say, the crowd transformed into a frenzied mass of maniacs with horned fists raised whilst bellowing for the band to hit the stage. The smoke machine was pumping, and then red lights shot up from between the monitors at the front of the stage. The entire band was instantly lit from below with a demonic glow as they smashed into their opening number, 'Fall from Grace', at skull-crushing volume. They hit the crowd like a steel leviathan. There was an intense, vehement, all-consuming ferocity to what was happening here. This even went beyond what I had seen at the Sabbat gig. But there again, this was full-throttle death metal being played by one of the best bands of that type on the planet!

They mixed tracks from their first two albums and tore the venue to pieces! The audience was like a boiling cauldron, with people being jettisoned over the top of the crowd and towards the stage with limbs flailing around in a near formless chaos of body parts. And I was right up for that. I tapped someone on the shoulder and gestured with an upwards indication towards the stage. I then braced myself for impact. I was shoved, lifted and hoisted up onto the top of the crowd, and bulldozed over people's heads towards the stage like a human torpedo in a hurricane-force gale. A bit of scrambling and grabbing and there I was: on stage at Rock City with Morbid Angel! *YEEAAHH!* Only one thing for it: take a running jump and dive back into the chaos!

I've often been asked: 'Isn't stage-diving dangerous? What if someone stuck their fist up in the air just as your face was plummeting down and smacked you in the eye? What if the seas parted just as you were taking a dive and you decked it – *splat* – onto the floor? What if you got a Doc Martens boot wrapped around your face? What if…?'

Well… yes. I suppose if any of those things were to happen, you would probably end up doubled over for a while, or possibly hospitalised with disfiguring injuries. But, on the whole, that never occurred. Most folk were fine. A bit knocked about maybe, but fine nevertheless. I bear no scars and I've never been in therapy on account of my actions. The thing is, you simply don't think about the consequences. You just catch onto the manic feel and energy of the gig and go stark staring bonkers!

But on the other hand, I did cop for it once. I was at a Sepultura gig, again at Rock City, in 1991, and I did my flying over the top of the crowd act. I was just about within reach of the stage when somebody absolutely lamped me in the right kidney. I don't know if it was a fist, an arm, an elbow or a boot. No idea. But my body turned into a huge sack of spuds. A security guard grabbed hold of me and pulled me over the barrier in front of the stage. He gave me a cursory look over, and then decided that I was adequately alive. I hobbled to the back of the hall and did my best to unkink the damage. God all flaming mighty, it hurt! It felt like my whole body had been lanced! I needed a few minutes… But then, guess what? Straight back into it. Adrenalin has a fantastic way of covering up pain!

Bolt Thrower	'Cenotaph'
Death	'Cosmic Sea'
	'Suicide Machine'
Deicide	'Dead but Dreaming'
Morbid Angel	'Fall From Grace'
	'Rebel Lands'
Napalm death	'If the Truth Be Known'
	'Unfit Earth'
Obituary	'Cause of Death'
Pestilence	'Stigmatized'
	'Twisted Truth'
Sadus	'Black'
	'The Wake'
Sepultura	'Dead Embryonic Cells'
	'Under Siege (Regnum Irae)'

CHAPTER 13

'I'LL FIGHT YOU ALL!'

But alongside this, there was also the madness which was Guns N' Roses.

It's hard to impress upon the younger generation just how massive Guns N' Roses really were, especially when they embarked on their tour for the *Use Your Illusion* albums. It is equally difficult to explain just how much carnage was left in their wake. Even before their debut album was released in 1987, there was a buzz of authentic unpredictability and danger about the band, and this especially applied to their vocalist, Axl Rose.

They dominated the front covers of the rock press, and were frequently at odds with the media, the establishment and whoever else encountered them. Their alcohol and drug consumption was truly legendary. Even the very nature of taking a *piss* was referred to as 'going for a G N' R' – a 'Slash', you see?

I'd first heard Guns N' Roses on the *Time to Rock* compilation which I had bought while I was at school, and I thought they sounded okay. Nothing out of the ordinary, but okay. But following that, and having heard their track 'Paradise City' on Tommy Vance's

Friday Rock Show, I became addicted! This band was not only playing absolutely savage music which in places bordered on punk, their lyrics were openly confrontational, and it was absolutely clear why only certain tracks could be released as singles. The second track on their album, *Appetite for Destruction*, contains a lyric with which the band cordially invites its listeners to FUCK OFF! This practically knocked the blocks off most listeners the first time they heard it. Even the likes of Mötley Crüe and W.A.S.P. hadn't come out with anything quite like that! And as for the final track on that album, 'Rocket Queen'? Well, just listen to the instrumental break in that one. You try getting that played on the radio!

But they were touring, and this was huge. This immense drug-addled wrecking ball was heading to England. They were also bringing Soundgarden and Faith No More with them as support. There was no acceptable way that I could miss this. There was an implicit obligation directed at metal fans that you be there. Andrew and I were dead set on going to the Manchester show at the Maine Road football stadium. He sorted out the tickets. Good man.

Not that Mum and Dad were all that impressed about me going. They'd heard the stories too. In fact, some of what had taken place at Guns N' Roses gigs had made it onto major network news. Two fans had been killed in the rush towards the stage during their Donington Monsters of Rock set in 1988, and there had been major incidents during other gigs sometimes resulting in full-scale riots.

I was undeterred. I'd be fine. Of course I was going. There was no question about that.

But I wasn't entirely sure that I believed myself. After all, I was openly and willingly walking into the jungle.

*

I went up to Manchester the day before the gig and stayed at Andrew's place. He was still living with some of his pals from his university days, and it was all pretty relaxed. There was beer aplenty, and a fridge full of snacks. And Andrew was handy in the kitchen, so we ate well. He had a cassette player that was set up to play the *Use Your Illusion II* album on a continuous loop. We were primed!

We headed out mid-afternoon on 14th June 1992 for the gig of our lives. The sun was shining and all was well. It was just a short walk to the stadium, and we grabbed a takeaway and a beer on the way. The area around the Maine Road Stadium was rammed with black T-shirt wearers. But it was far from just G N' R fans, or fans of their type of music, that were going to this gig. T-shirts were, and always will be, a clear indication through which people's tastes can be seen. This is particularly the case with metal fans. We could clearly see fans of Maiden, Anthrax, Megadeth, Poison, Overkill, and others. There were also crowds of death metal fans, punk fans and goths. Additionally, there were quite a few Rolling Stones, R.E.M. and U2 T-shirt wearers hanging around. In short, this was a massive gathering of people who were fans of a huge range of genres, some of them nothing to do with heavy metal of any kind. There was a real sense of community. Guns N' Roses were bringing the world together. What a great bunch of guys!

Beers chugged, we pointed ourselves at Maine Road. The stadium's normal use as the home of the Manchester City football team took second place today. We could hear music blasting out of the PA system well before we squeezed through the tight and clanking turnstiles. And then we were in. Amazing! The place was huge, a gigantic amphitheatre, and it was alive with anticipation. It was filling up quickly.

A quick G N' R...

And onwards to the merchandise store.

This was metal merchandising like I'd never seen in my life. It wasn't just a stall with a couple of blokes behind it; this was a full-on shop. There were several different T-shirts for all three bands playing that day, but also programmes, back patches, and little pins which could be stuck into lapels. This was definitely the way to replenish a wardrobe.

The stage itself was incredible. For one thing, it was vast. There were huge banners to the left and right which reached from the floor all the way up to the lighting rigs. They showed massive prints of the *Use Your Illusion* album covers. There were amps all along the back of the stage. There were ramps, raised sections, and an elevated area for the drum riser. There was also a very conspicuous-looking amp sitting right in the middle of the stage. On it was daubed the word 'DUFF'. Presumably this was a bass bin.

This was big league stuff!

We shuffled our way into the middle of the crowd and got in front of the mixing desk. It was a great spot. We had a wide-angle view of the whole stage. Rock music continued to pour through the air, but now the volume had been rammed up, and the thousands-strong crowd was starting to get lively.

Then, all of a sudden, a roar came from the front of the crowd. Soundgarden's drummer was behind the kit and was pointing his sticks into the air. Horned fists were raised in unison and the vast crowd bellowed its approval. Then on came Chris Cornell leading the rest of the band. God! This was happening right now, and I was a part of it! This was the most awesome thing ever! I'd never really heard any Soundgarden at that point, but that didn't bother me. I was on a wave and I was riding it like a pro. They cranked out the tunes for about forty or so minutes, and then disappeared backstage. I looked at Andrew. Andrew looked at me. We were both sporting Cheshire cat grins. Yup, no question. Soundgarden had kicked ass and had set the pace!

The PA music came back on again, this time much louder than it had been before Soundgarden had started their set.

Then, after a short interval, the crowd roared again and on

came Faith No More. They were right on form. They went for it and blasted through a fantastic set which was heavy on the hits and got the crowd bouncing. There were fists in the air and the audience was screaming out the lyrics to the tracks. This was stunning. I'd never heard bass like that before in my life, and Jim Martin's chugging guitar was as solid as a rock. Faith No More practically made the ground rumble! Andrew and I were both fans and we engaged full mosh mode with heads banging, sweat flying, and horned fists raised. The band pumped their way through numbers such as 'The Real Thing', 'From Out of Nowhere', 'We Care a Lot', and the interestingly titled 'Jizzlobber'.

Of course, there were weird moments. This was Faith No More after all. A gig of theirs would not be right without a little bit of 'strange'. Partway through their set, Mike Patton grabbed hold of a large black bin bag. He then walked up to the front of the stage and started talking about the planet and ecology, and how you should 'bin your shit'.

They finished off with a brilliant version of 'Epic', and then they disappeared.

Amazing! What a rush! What a day! The entire stadium was sizzling! And next we were going to get Guns N' Roses! What would they be like live? We'd heard stories about crazy gigs, hellacious drug habits and volatile temperamental outbursts during shows. We just wanted to get stuck right into this gig and take a direct burst of G N' R insanity.

That said, we knew that Axl Rose was a bit unreliable when it came to watching the clock. It was wishful thinking to imagine that the band would show up on time. There was no point in expecting anything even resembling punctuality.

Of course, there was always the possibility of chaos, and that it could just be a shambolic train wreck. Axl might just throw his toys out of the pram and storm off stage mid set. It was always possible that the band might not show up at all. Buying a ticket for a Guns

N' Roses show was a bit like making a bet on which you had no idea of the odds of things like this happening.[3] But of one thing you could be certain: if they were in fact there, the core band members would all be utterly loaded on whatever narcotic goodies might have been available backstage to ingest one way or another.

So we waited.

And waited.

And we waited some more, thousands of us in the red-hot sun.

Well, maybe there was a problem behind the scenes. This was a huge gig, and everything would need to be set up properly before the band hit the stage. But this was a bit much. People all around us were swigging out of bottles, mopping sweat from their reddening faces and generally starting to get onto the 'pissed-off scale'. Faith No More's set was drifting off into the past and now seemed like a distant memory. The minutes ticked by, and then an hour passed. What was going on? Was it even worth hanging around? If anything, waiting around like this was just plain boring. The energy of the afternoon had dissipated completely, and now the huge crowd was rapidly getting more and more hacked off.

One guy, just off to my right, lost it. 'Fuck 'em! I've had enough! I'm never going to listen to this band ever again! I'm going to smash all of the albums of theirs that I've bought!'

And he was gone.

And then another guy who was standing right in front of me: 'Shit, I've got to go. I'll miss my train because of these bastards!' He ripped up his ticket and threw the pieces up into the air. He shrugged his shoulders, flipped the bird at the stage, and disappeared.

The whole crowd was now starting to get rowdy. There was a general sense of anger flowing around the stadium like a Mexican wave. There were boos, catcalls, things being thrown. A real

---

3   Just to add an extra layer of unpredictability to Guns N' Roses, this gig fell on a rescheduled date. It had originally been planned for 9th June, but, for reasons which were never made all that clear, that date was ditched...

atmosphere of hostility was starting to build.

It looked like things were going to get nasty. Were we going to be stuck in the middle of yet another newsworthy shitstorm? It wouldn't take much to set off this powder keg. If a message were to come through saying that the gig was off, thousands of people were set to spontaneously combust with rage!

And still… we… waited.

I leaned in towards Andrew and said, 'They could probably have finished their set before they even started it, if they're even going to come on at all. Why the hell are they doing this? What a waste of time! What do you reckon? Should we just fuck off as well?'

It didn't seem like a bad option.

But just then, a breakthrough. The tone of the crowd's mood changed, and the first chord of 'Nightrain' blasted out at us. Thank Christ for that! The band *was* actually in the building.

But the crowd didn't exactly rise with approval. If anything, its anger now had a focus, and this fury exploded with a massive chorus of booing and a huge rush towards the stage. Andrew and I grabbed hold of each other and just went with the human barrage braced for whatever might hit us. God alone knew what the security guards in front of the stage were thinking. To be honest, I think they must have been shitting bricks! The crowd crashed forward and kept going. I didn't see anybody go down, but there were hundreds of accidents waiting to happen right there. It was undoubtedly a close call for a lot of folk.

The band tore through their first track and gradually got the audience on side. From being enraged out of frustration and annoyance, the mood of the crowd switched to a controlled anger that matched the music which was being flung at it. This must have been the most dangerous crowd I had ever been caught up in. You really had to watch yourself!

And the music didn't let up. Axl's ear-splitting screams during 'Live and Let Die' were almost enough to shake out your fillings and burst your eyeballs! Bloody hell! How could anybody do that? This guy must have had pipes of cast iron! The band carried on relentlessly. Then bass-wielding Duff McKagan fronted 'Attitude', originally by the Misfits, which was a no-holds-barred punk number.

I'm sure both Andrew and I had taken a few body-blows by now, and it was hardly surprising. This was as much a full-frontal attack as it was a gig! The band was out, guns blazing, howitzers booming, and screw the collateral. If you were quite close to the stage, as we were now, then this was a gig to be survived. We did get a breather when they played 'Patience', but then something happened which really stood out above everything we'd seen and heard up until then. Slash strode up to the front of the stage, shirt off and hair everywhere as usual, and started playing a solo. Fair enough. This was true to form. But then he switched the mood of the solo to something which sounded vaguely familiar. What was that tune? I recognised it from somewhere, but I couldn't place it. Then Andrew turned to me with an amazed expression on his face:

'Fuck me! He's playing the theme from *The Godfather!*'

'Fuck me! So he is!'

And it was an accompanied solo. The entire band joined him. Genius! No two ways about it!

Then they powered onwards, cranking out classic after classic. And Axl was throwing himself around on stage like an uncontrollable psychopath! It was as though he was baiting the crowd – 'COME ON THEN! YEAH! THE LOT OF YOU! *I'LL FIGHT YOU ALL!*'

Guns N' Roses played for about two hours and gave the crowd a non-stop, unapologetic, taboo-laden bombardment. By the end, after the crowd had turned borderline genocidal during 'Paradise City', a lot of the audience looked just plain gobsmacked, as well as heavily mauled. For a lot of people, it looked like they'd experienced more than just a gig; it looked more like they'd survived a battlefield.

But holy crap, we were thirsty! What with all the waiting around, and the sun which had been beating down, we were parched. Fortunately, that area of Manchester was well supplied with pubs. Most of them were jam-packed with people who had got out of the stadium before us, but it didn't take us too long before we got to the brass taps. Pints disappeared down our necks effortlessly. Sinking those beers was like feasting on a long, strong hit of life. And we were already high from the gig. It had been mad, chaotic at times, but the musical savagery that had battered us that day hit the spot dead centre. Guns N' Roses ruled!

So yes: carnage, unpredictability and flat-out danger. That was what you got with Guns N' Roses. But who cared? We'd been there and done it. We'd experienced the jungle and lived!

*

But there was another connection to the G N' R tour which I didn't find out about until a while later. Rob, who was a massive fan, had recently joined the army, having left school at sixteen. He had actually signed up at the recruitment office next door to Way Ahead Records in Derby. Rob had been even less interested in school than me. At least I *turned up* for my exams! As it was, he did his basic training at Pirbright Barracks and passed with flying colours.

One morning he was out on a barrack square with his pals and a tetchy-looking NCO was giving them an eyeballing. The sergeant walked up and down the ranks a couple of times and suddenly barked out: 'Right, which ones of you are interested in music?' There were a few nervous shuffles in case any suggestion of enthusiasm might mean having to shift a grand piano or something else equally uninviting. 'I'm waiting for volunteers, and I'm expecting at least...'

Then Rob belted out: 'Okay, sir!'

'Who was that?'

'Kerr, sir!'

'Right then, Kerr. You.' The NCO shot a quick look across a row of faces which were all trying not to make eye contact. 'And you, you, and you! I want to see you all in my office as soon as we've finished here!'

The 'volunteers' all headed in the direction of the office with a collective feeling of *Oh, sweet Jesus Christ! What the fuck have we let ourselves in for now?*

Next, the briefing.

The sergeant started off: 'Okay then, now that we're out of the way of that lot, I'll tell you what's going on. You have all just volunteered to take part in a security operation in the north of London.'

Oh shoot, what's coming...?

'There will be multiple agencies involved, and the army is required to take part.'

Come on, tell us the worst. Just get on with it...

'You are going to be front line security at the Guns N' Roses gig at Wembley Stadium tomorrow. You will be standing at the front of the stage, facing the crowd, and checking for any shenanigans. Understand?'

There was a huge collective sigh of relief followed by a feeling of *Holy fuck! Did we just hit the best jackpot in town*? Up front security for Guns N' Roses at Wembley Stadium with the likely chance of backstage access. Rob glanced across at his mates. Their faces were all split with huge grins. The morning had certainly taken a turn for the better.

So, there he was in front of the stage at Wembley with Guns N' Roses cranking out their show to the massive heaving crowd. And as for facing the crowd and checking for said shenanigans? Balls to that, Sarge! He spent most of the time watching the gig from the best spot in the venue!

Death	'Secret Face'
Dream Theater	'Pull Me Under'
Faith No More	'Epic'
	'From Out of Nowhere'
	'We Care a Lot'
Guns N' Roses	'Civil War'
	'Coma'
	'Right Next Door to Hell'
Megadeth	'Symphony of Destruction'
Metallica	'Through the Never'
	'Wherever I May Roam'
Soundgarden	'Jesus Christ Pose'
	'Rusty Cage'
W.A.S.P.	'Arena of Pleasure'
	'The Idol'

CHAPTER 14

Straight down the middle metal

Trends come, and trends go. Some things come into favour, fall out, and then come back in again. Like flares. Having said that, certain things defy any attempt by fashion, marketing, or popular opinion to knock them off track. There were, and still are, some bands that simply couldn't care less what the flavour of the month might be; they dig in and defend their territory whatever else may be going on. These are the exponents of what I call 'straight down the middle metal'.

As the 1990s went on, metal music became marginalised in many places. The UK was one of them. Bands like Blur, Pulp, the Stone Roses (I quite liked them too), and Suede were now the big players, whereas metal bands were becoming viewed as a thing of the remote past. Some people were even starting to view them as being fossilised in antediluvian sediments. From out of Seattle emerged grunge. And this proceeded to steamroller its way through the metal scene, upending much of what had seemed to be so permanent and enduring. Complex riffing was out; guitar solos as we had come to understand and love them were out as well. Everything was stripped down and simplified. And it all sounded so damned miserable!

Some metal bands unquestionably fell by the wayside and got ditched by their record companies. This certainly happened to Wolfsbane, despite their second album, *Down Fall the Good Guys*, being genuinely fantastic. And what did *Kerrang!* say about the album? Five K's. Quite right too. This was one of the best albums I had heard in ages. There was a brightness and immediacy to every single track, and the guitar solos and choruses were unreservedly shit hot!

But it didn't seem to matter. Young bands like these were getting dropped left, right, and centre, and no matter how promising they might have sounded in theory, many ended up going nowhere in practice. Some bands tried to change their style to fit in with the times, which, more often than not, didn't work. Xentrix called it a day, as did Sabbat. True metal fans found themselves in lumber wondering what the hell had happened to their beloved music. The Donington Monsters of Rock festival sputtered to a halt, as did the *Headbangers Ball*. Even Way Ahead Records, my alma mater, ceased to be. After metal's astronomical run through the 1980s, the scene was now taking a massive and very sudden crash dive.

There was no question about it. The beast was limping!

Metal bands were starting to fragment, and tried, tested, and proven methods associated with set line-ups were now being cast asunder. Even Iron Maiden was a victim: Bruce Dickinson, the vocalist I had first heard screaming out the lyrics from *The Number of the Beast* album, was gone, as was long-time guitarist Adrian Smith. Rob Halford left Judas Priest, and Mötley Crüe fired Vince Neil and lost the plot completely. The metal scene in the 1990s was a complete shambles. Many bands had turned into warring factions. It wasn't clear whether any of them even knew what they were doing any more. Van Halen was disintegrating, and the focus of their music was becoming so blurred that it seemed as though they were just going to end in ignominious chaos. It was sad to see. On top of this, in 2004, the movie *Metallica: Some*

Kind of Monster, much of which showed fly-on-the-wall footage of the band, indicated just how bad things could get even amongst the members of one of the most successful bands in the world. Metallica was holding together by the skin of its teeth, but it was hardly the band I had got to know in years past. Their frazzled and demoralised state of burnout was self-evident. And as for Guns N' Roses – well, who could say?

There were also a number of tragedies within the metal scene which shouldn't be overlooked. In 1991, Steve Clarke, who had been a member of Def Leppard since 1978, passed away at the age of thirty in the wake of alcohol addiction. Ingo Schwichtenberg, who had been an original member of Helloween, also died. He had been suffering from complex mental health problems for some time, and in the spring of 1995, at the age of just twenty-nine, he committed suicide. Additionally, in the summer of 1999, Chuck Schuldiner, of the band Death, was diagnosed with a brain tumour. Within two years, and at the age of thirty-four, he passed away.

Events such as these were terrible, and they were also great levellers. At that point in my life, I tended to look at things with the wide-eyed naivety of the young, and I breezed through without really considering mortality. And why should mortality apply to rock stars anyway? These guys were invincible and could handle anything the world might throw at them. But, in reality, they weren't and they couldn't. They were only human, just like you and me, and sadly some of them were more breakable than others.

*

A lot of 'fans' switched sides during the 1990s too. One Saturday night, I was up at the Rockhouse in Derby when a Guns N' Roses track came on. A couple of years earlier, the whole club would have gone crazy for it, but now the track was viewed as a bit *passé*. I remarked to a pal of mine that this was one of those tracks to get up for, but he had completely lost interest in it. To him it was yesterday's tired old news. 'Sweet Child of Mine' was blasting out of the speakers, but he and his mates were just sitting there with stony faces, cropped hair and droopy fags, looking detached and disinterested. It made me wonder why they'd bothered to turn up to the club at all.

It really hacked me off!

As for me, well, maybe I was out of sync with the times. But so what if I was? I knew what I liked and there was no way I was going to compromise on that. I had never thought that, whilst only in my twenties, I would need to start reminiscing about the 'good old days'.

Saying that you were a metal fan in the 1990s had different connotations as well. It would imply, to the uninitiated, that you were into stuff like Korn or Slipknot or Linkin Park. Nu metal and metalcore were becoming the things to be into. Apparently. There were lots of occasions when I had to clarify my position to people, who were often younger than me, concerning metal. They would be going on about Limp Bizkit and I would actually have to step in and stop them: 'No, no, no, mate. What I mean is real metal, true metal, ACTUAL HEAVY METAL! Do you *know* what I'm talking about?' Often, they seemed not to. Either that or they looked at me as if I was plankton.

It was a little dispiriting.

But, like I say, there were a number of bands out there that simply didn't care what the trends were. Grunge could be hitting from one side, rap from another, and indie from yet another. But these bands rammed on ahead regardless and unapologetically. A few bands that spring to mind are Motörhead, AC/DC and Manowar. There was no room for compromise where they were concerned, and you wouldn't have expected it of them anyway. You could absolutely rely on them. These guys basically cut through trends like cheese wire: in a direct line, straight down the middle.

Motörhead was a phenomenon. They weren't hemmed in by any fads. Lemmy didn't even define the band as heavy metal. He preferred to call Motörhead's music rock 'n' roll. But, that being said, it was heavy and fast enough for most metal fans, Hell's Angels, and a lot of punks to view the band and its music with a kind of *we're not worthy* reverence. Musically, Lemmy did precisely what he wanted throughout his career, and he didn't care whom he offended. He just blasted onwards on his own terms, consistently giving the middle finger to naysayers whoever they might have been.

And they were hardly a subtle band. Motörhead gigs were known for being deafeningly loud. I saw them at the Carling Academy in Glasgow when they were touring *The Wörld Is Yours*, and by the end of the show, my friends and I were standing outside the venue as part of a larger group listening to them playing 'Overkill' as their last encore. The volume inside the venue was like shellfire set to blast forests into splinters. It was literally unbearable!

The thing about Motörhead was that they simply played one kind of music, and that kind of music was, well, Motörhead. Be they fast tracks, slower tracks, bluesy numbers, or even dabblings with acoustic songs, their style could only be defined by their name. They created their own bracket and they alone could stand within it. Their banner was unique. They were revered for their to-hell-with-it attitude and the bluntness of their delivery. If they had a point to make, they were sure to make it. They even released an album entitled *Bastards*! They were loud to the point of sheer violence, and took issues like war, politics, current affairs and religion in their stride, with an approach which most bands would never dare attempt. And, of course, hedonism was spelt out and underlined throughout. There were no hidden meanings or innuendoes to be found in Lemmy's lyrics. Take tracks like 'Jailbait', 'Love Me Like a Reptile', and 'Vibrator'. See what I mean? And Lemmy didn't take criticism lying down either. A journalist once went up to him and said, 'Hey, Lemmy, you've only ever written one song in your life really, haven't you?' To which he replied, 'Yeah, just like Chuck Berry. *And they were all good!*'

As for AC/DC and sticking to their guns, they weren't likely to shift their ground either and they never attempted to fall into line with any trends. Like with Motörhead, you could never mistake an AC/DC track for anything by any other band. Malcolm Young's rhythm playing and Phil Rudd's drumming were a unique combination, and as for Brian Johnson's shrieking vocals, the whole sound was unmistakeable. From the first time I heard them up in Andrew's room at St. Hugh's, right up to date, they have never really changed. You know exactly what to expect from them. The production on their albums may have polished up their sound a bit, but, essentially, with AC/DC you get about twelve tracks per album: five about drinking, five about shagging, and the other two about rock 'n' roll. I once saw a televised interview with Brian Johnson in which he was asked about the nature of AC/DC's lyrics. In his usual cheerful manner, he put things quite succinctly: 'Aye, that's reet! We're a durty band!' Listen to 'Girl's Got Rhythm', 'Let's Get It Up', and 'Caught with your Pants Down'. That's consistency.

And what about Manowar? Well, what can you say? You can't get any more metal than that! Not only were they in the habit of playing deafening sets which went on for up to three hours, their metal credentials were absolutely cast in polished steel. Just about every song they wrote was either to do with metal, fighting for metal, dying for metal, or something to do with warriors performing valiant deeds in the name of (what else?) metal! They weren't going to let grunge intimidate them. No, no! Their 1992 album, *The Triumph of Steel*, contained tracks such as 'Metal Warriors', 'The Power of thy Sword', and the unbelievably over the top 'Achilles, Agony and Ecstasy in Eight Parts', which clocked in at over twenty-eight minutes. Also, check out 'Battle Hymn' and 'Hail and Kill'. If those tracks don't have you donning armour, grabbing the biggest sword you can find, and sprinting at your enemies going *GAAAAAHH!*, then frankly, my friend, you don't have a pulse.

And take a look at their album covers. They are packed with images of flashing steel, lightning bolts, and pectorals you would need a rope and harness to scale!

This was all fine.

But many other metal bands were slipping into obscurity. The general mood of the 1990s suggested that they had outlived their usefulness and that extinction should be quietly accepted. For the most part, metal gigs for the genuinely faithful were getting smaller and smaller. Bands that had recently been playing arenas were now playing the club circuit and hoping that their true fans, their follow-you-anywhere fans, were going to turn up to shows.

There are a lot of disgruntled metal fans out there who still say that it was all down to Nirvana, and insist that the grunge movement that they headed killed metal. They see 'Smells Like Teen Spirit' as the death knell of the metal scene, and single out Kurt Cobain with teeth-gritted finger-pointing disdain. Their view is that he was responsible for casting the metal gods into the chasm of irrelevance and obscurity. For a while I felt the same way. I felt justifiably pissed off.

But thinking about it now?

Cobblers! I simply couldn't picture any conspiratorial plot within the Nirvana camp aimed at bringing on the demise of metal. There's no way I could envision a scene involving Kurt Cobain gathering his bandmates together and explaining to them that their purpose was to seal the tomb of heavy metal forever and fling it into the nether regions of oblivion. Where the record company that signed Nirvana was concerned, well, that would have been a different matter. They saw how big that band could become. They would have been the ones pulling the strings, and the way Nirvana, and similar bands, were constantly promoted on MTV, on radio stations, and in clubs made it clear that the times were indeed a-changing. Things had moved on. Metal had suddenly become old news.

*

Or had it?

There was definitely something going on somewhere.

And that somewhere was Scandinavia. In this partially arctic area of Northern Europe, things were actually looking up as the 1990s began. Scandinavia was becoming a breeding ground for a multitude of new bands, and grunge had no impact on them whatsoever. In 1991, Therion and Unleashed released their debut albums, as did others. This was strictly confined to the underground, but if you knew where to look (and as you know, I had my sources), you could find albums by these bands cropping up in the shops. The committed metal fan couldn't help but be curious about these emerging sounds. Then other bands started to emerge: Sonata Arctica, Apocalyptica, Dimmu Borgir...

Of course, some Scandinavian bands such as King Diamond and Entombed had been going strong since the 1980s, and they just kept on going. Whilst at school, I bought a copy of King Diamond's *The Eye*, and I couldn't get enough of it. The album's story of a seventeenth century witch trial was based on real events, and, of course, being a historian with an enduring interest in the darker passages of time, I had to go delving into the deeper details. King's knack for storytelling was fantastic, and Andy LaRocque's guitar playing was up there with the best.

But one thing stood out as strange in the 1990s. And that was Pantera. As soon as their *Cowboys from Hell* album crushed its way onto the airwaves, they instantaneously became massive in metal circles. They were, as far as a lot of people were concerned, new. I thought they were... They had, in fact, been around since the start of the 1980s, but their glam metal phase hadn't really hit

142

home. It took a change of personnel and a change of style and – *wallop!* A slavering monster was born! And not only that, they were becoming huge. They were hitting the mainstream – in the *1990s*? *Seriously*? Most other metal bands had been forced to take a back seat. But Pantera's attack was so furious and unrelenting, they simply brooked no opposition. They were loose and on a savage mission, and when they released *Vulgar Video*, this just went to show how outrageous this foursome really was. And as for their fans, they were practically fixated. Dimebag Darrell was a god in their eyes!

But there was more than just this. Although metal had largely skulked away in many places, the 1990s was incubating a number of brand-new bands which would make a huge global impact as the new millennium dawned and would prove to cut straight down the middle, blasting the popular musical fads into shards both left and right. It was my brother, Rob, who eloquently underscored this point for me. He called me up one day: 'Jesus! Phil! Have you heard of the Black Label Society? Fucking hell, you've got to listen to this shit!'

At the time I hadn't, but Rob proceeded to fill me in, chapter and verse. He was a huge Ozzy fan and had basically followed Zakk Wylde's guitar playing note for note and pinch harmonic for pinch harmonic ever since the *No Rest for the Wicked* album. I was also well acquainted with Mr Wylde's form, as I was, quite justifiably, also heavily into Ozzy Osbourne at that point.

Rob went on: 'Man, you've *got* to hear this band! The guitar playing is *fucking sick!* Check this out!' He then stuck his phone right up against one of his stereo speakers and blasted out something from the *Sonic Brew* album.

Well now, what was this? Rob unquestionably had a point. Zakk and his band blasted their way onto the scene like TNT! He riffed like a tyrant and he could shred as well as anyone I had ever heard. If ever there was a guy who could bring metal back to the masses after the stammering 1990s, then this was the dude. Something had definitely awoken, and it was set to bite and slash with all the attitude of a psychotic Cerberus!

And, on top of that:

Bruce Dickinson and Adrian Smith rejoined Iron Maiden.

Vince Neil rejoined Mötley Crüe.

Rob Halford rejoined Judas Priest.

The beast was back!

Accept	'Balls to the Wall'
AC/DC	'For Those About to Rock'
Black Sabbath	'Neon Knights'
Dio	'Breathless'
Exodus	'Blacklist'
Iron Maiden	'Where Eagles Dare'
Judas Priest	'The Sentinel'
Kreator	'Phobia'
Manowar	'Battle Hymn'
Motörhead	'Bomber'
Onslaught	'The Devil's Legion'
Ozzy Osbourne	'Old L.A. Tonight'
Slayer	'Criminally Insane'
The Scorpions	'Blackout'
Therion	'Birth of Venus Illegitima'

CHAPTER 15

'Not in our neighbourhood!'

A few years ago, this happened to me.

I was heading back home with Mum. We'd been to town, and I was helping her carry some shopping. As we got onto our street, a neighbour from a few doors down appeared, and we stopped for a chat, as you do. We just talked about this and that, inconsequential stuff really, and then we went on our way and I thought nothing more of it. Until a few days later. I'd been out to town by myself, probably music hunting, and I was kitted out in my usual black gear. I was heading home by the normal route when I saw this neighbour again. She was on the same side of the street and some distance away, and I noticed her before she spotted me. I was thinking we could have a bit of a chinwag and pick things up from where we'd left off last time. Just then, she looked up and saw me. Having realised I was there, she visibly hesitated and looked around, as though for an escape route. Rather than a fairly genial human being, what she saw was a hideous, demonic creature slithering towards her, bent on her damnation. I mean, come on, give me a break! She checked for traffic, and then scurried across the road. She kept her head and eyes facing directly ahead, as though blinkered, as she passed me by on the other side. Then, when she'd determined that a safe distance had opened up between us, she checked over her shoulder and crossed to my side of the road again.

Well, fuck me, readers! How about *that*?

But I'm sure this kind of thing happens quite a lot, probably more than we're aware of, and that I'm not the only one who's experienced it.

Wolfsbane summed up this sort of reaction to heavy metal fans nicely in their track 'The Loveless'. They hit the nail on the head and flattened it out. The lyrics in that track rang true with me when I first heard them just as they do now.

Basically, the situation is this:

There's a certain kind of person out there, and I'm sure we've all run into them from time to time, who, at the very idea of heavy metal music, react with a kind of sour-faced gag reflex. You know the type? Yep, I'll bet. They consider it to be beneath them and claim that they wouldn't be seen *dead* associated with anything attached to heavy metal. Ooh, the *very idea!* Goths get similar grief, as do punks, but we'll stick with metal for the time being.

Their perception is that it is best not to encourage any kind of interest in heavy metal, as it's not really an appropriate medium to be associated with polite society. They view metal as being connected to sinister left-hand paths which could only lead to shadowy sectors of best avoided subcultures; that it's beneath-the-trapdoor music that emanates from murky places, and that the entrance to this chasm really should be closed and sealed for the benefit of more enlightened folk.

In other words, they would rather dismiss heavy metal music out of hand than engage constructively in any discussion on the subject.

It's actually quite sad when you think about it.

People like this are completely missing the point. I'm no sociologist, but in my experience metal fans come from practically every walk of life and social strata there is. Not only that, they are, in themselves, a multigenerational global phenomenon, not just a bunch of hairy tattooed kids who, from behind twitching curtains, are told that they don't look the part: 'not in our neighbourhood!'

I'll give you a good example of what I mean:

I went to see Judas Priest whilst they were touring their *Angel of Retribution* album. At one point during the gig, a child of about ten or so years old was hoisted onto, presumably, her dad's shoulders in order to get a better view from the pit. Following the track the band had been playing, Rob Halford singled out the child and addressed her personally. He pointed out that the band would have formed way before her parents had even met, but that this kid was now part of the new generation of fans. 'Welcome to the metal family. Whoever you are, you're one of us!'

That's the way it should be.

The music certainly doesn't discriminate, but, apparently, discriminating people do.

The fact of the matter is that metal music, and the whole culture associated with it, is like a massive family with generation upon generation embracing the same culture and welcoming in new members with open arms. It's actually extremely communal. Granted, this is the case with lots of other kinds of music as well, but why single out heavy metal for the lash?

*

And there certainly were heavy lashes out there. In the 1980s, pressure groups such as the PMRC started popping up in the USA, and their message was, essentially, that rock and metal music were agents for the corruption of the young, and that certain lyrical messages and associated imagery should be banned. They even published a list of fifteen tracks, referred to as '*The Filthy Fifteen*', which they deemed 'dangerous' for one reason or another. The criteria for their criticism generally revolved around references to sex, drugs, alcohol and the occult. Well, you can find all of these things in just about any kind of music if you go looking. Take a look at country music, jazz and gangster rap. Even audience members at Niccolò Paganini's recitals in nineteenth century Italy swore blind that they could see the Devil's image guiding the violinist's hands. It's safe to say that there was quite a lot of hysteria on the loose. Ironically, this actually served to draw attention to the very thing the PMRC so abhorred, and the opposite of what they intended occurred: sales of albums rocketed. So, more fool them really! But it wasn't just metal that they were hacking away at: Madonna, Cindy Lauper and Prince also featured on their list. But no one focused too closely on them, especially when the Judas Priest trial hit the headlines in 1990.

Also, it always seemed strange to me that *The Filthy Fifteen* did not include anything written by Alice Cooper or Ted Nugent. Maybe the Washington Wives were closet fans...

Music videos produced by metal bands picked up on this kind of criticism as well. They were often used to show how fans of the music could be singled out, often by parental figures, and told to, effectively, grow up and grow out of it. The video for 'Peace Sells' by Megadeth is a good example of this. Also, Poison often started their videos using a scene looking at the sniping that took place towards themselves and their fans. And as for Twisted Sister, well, Mr Snider really knew how to address matters! Ozzy also took on the critics and right wing religious objectors in the track 'Rock 'n' Roll Rebel', but Blackie Lawless really nailed it. When, in the track 'I'm Alive', he screams out to be left alone, you can tell he genuinely means it.

And there was another thing that used to make me cringe. There were certain TV presenters in the UK who took a patronising line when it came to showing anything related to metal on their shows. It was as though they just wanted to make jocular excuses for playing a video or showing a performance. W.A.S.P. were given a half-hour slot on the BBC in 1986 whilst they were touring the *Inside the Electric Circus* album. There was nothing unusual about that: lots of bands were given similar opportunities to perform live on prime-time TV. And they played a really good set; brief, certainly shorter than a regular gig, but good nevertheless. However, it seems as though the mission of the TV presenters was to denigrate the show from the outset by making hilarious quips at the band's expense. Even as the gig ended, the presenter in the studio, rather than saying anything about the band, merely said, 'Now you can turn the volume on your TV sets back up.' It bugged me back then, and it still bugs me now when I look at those old videos on YouTube.

*

Another frequent refrain from detractors is that metal music is 'just noise and screaming', that 'it's not real music', and that 'it all sounds the same'. (Mutter, mutter, for Christ's sake save us... Mumble, mumble, could you seriously credit these tosspots...? Snarl, groan, there are none so deaf as those who will not hear...) Honestly, you can't seriously be telling me that Saxon, Metallica and Nightwish are non-musicians, and that all they have ever produced just merges together into a great muffled fog!

Okay, pull up your beverage of choice and get comfortable.

Where to start?

First principles, I think.

Learning to play any musical instrument is tough (and sometimes pretty expensive too, as I found out whilst searching around for guitars in Derby), especially if you want to play it really well. This could apply to the guitar, bass, drums, keyboards, or whatever. My first lesson, when I strolled up to my guitar teacher with a *Number of the Beast* songbook in one hand and a cheap classical guitar in the other, just showed me how far I had to go before I would be ready and confident enough to get up on a stage and stick it to a crowd. You have to be committed and prepared to *persist* and *persist* and *persist*. If you do, chances are you could become a good player, certainly good enough for jamming out cover tracks with a band.

And the inspiration behind metal music comes from right across the board as well. Blues is obviously right up there, especially when you look at guitar solos, but if you dig deeper you find blatant classical influences (Deep Purple, Randy Rhoads, Trans-Siberian Orchestra), or alternately jazz (Atheist, Dream Theater, Transatlantic), or even opera (Nightwish, Luca Turilli's Rhapsody, Within Temptation). Therion, from Sweden, perform with an array of soprano, tenor and bass vocalists. They've even written an actual, legitimate, opera!

These are technical influences, *really* technical influences. The bands that get up on stage and play tracks, or even full sets, which are based on such backgrounds aren't just musicians, they are the modern virtuosos. They are people who have studied, drilled and perfected their techniques to the point of being true exponents of them. In all honesty, hats off to these people. They're streets ahead of where I've got to!

Some of the more extreme metal bands can also be disarmingly melodic. Andy LaRocque's lyrical playing on the instrumental King Diamond track 'Insanity' is a fantastic example of this. Listen to the acoustic guitar playing in the Morbid Angel track 'Desolate Ways'. Who would have expected a death metal band to come up with something like that? And what about Quorthon's epic introduction to the Bathory track 'Shores in Flames'?

How any of this could be interpreted as non-musical beats the living daylights out of me! It simply underlines the point that some people genuinely don't know what they're talking about.

But, as is always the case with music, sometimes you come across something weird, with influences which seem so left field, that you wonder if you'd only imagined it. I was at Rock City in Nottingham with Richard, a pal of mine whom I'd met whilst resitting my A levels at Mackworth College in Derby, and it would have been at some point in 2004. We had bought tickets to see Jizzy Pearl, who had been the lead vocalist with Love/Hate. He'd put out a solo album called *Just a Boy* and was on tour. Neither of us planned on missing a gig like that! So, there we were. But when we arrived at the venue something seemed to be a bit out of joint. As I walked up the steps towards the main door, I hesitated and looked back at Richard. I asked him, 'Are you absolutely one hundred per cent certain we've come on the right night?'

Richard briefly stopped on the steps, his hair flapping in the breeze, and took a look at the ticket in his hand. 'I think so. Yep: date, venue, time, Love/Hate.[4] That's what it says on here.'

'I thought so, yeah. But listen to that. Does that sound normal to you?'

The reason for hesitancy was that, far from rock or metal issuing from the venue, we appeared to have arrived at some kind of ceilidh. Was there a Scottish music convention taking place at Rock City that night? Something certainly sounded out of place.

As we made our way through to the gig room, there was a distinct sound of drums and bagpipes. I've got nothing against that. But streaming out of a metal venue in the Midlands? That was a bit of a head-scratcher.

When we got there, we saw on stage a band which looked like no other band we had ever seen. Fair enough, there was a vocalist, a guitarist, bass player and drummer. They were heaving out riffs, and that all made perfect sense. However, backing them up and standing in front of the amp stacks were two of the biggest blokes

---

4   Even though Jizzy Pearl released *Just a boy* as a solo album, he was still touring under the band name, Love/Hate.

evolution seemed capable of creating. And they were both blasting out on bagpipes! Long hair, long beards, kilts, the works! We just stood there gawping for a while. What the heck was going on here?

Richard and I grabbed a couple of beers and watched from the bar. The band had the audience on side, and they were drilling their way through their set. In none of the tracks were there any guitar solos. The solo privilege was entirely in the domain of the pipers, and I don't think anyone was likely to step on their toes! Obviously, we didn't know any of the songs they were playing, but it hardly mattered; we just stood there in rapt fascination. But they did finish off with a track that really stood out. This one was called 'Drink and Fight', and it was basically about getting wrecked and causing a rumpus. The band sounded well experienced.

And they were damn good.

When they were done I asked someone who they were. The Mudmen, apparently, and they came not from the Scottish Highlands but from Canada. Right. You live and learn, don't you? I later sought out a couple of their albums. I still listen to them to this day.

Next, Jizzy Pearl and his band got up and played a set of straight-ahead metal. They got the joint jumping. This was normal service resuming, but it just goes to show that you need to keep an open mind because you never know what you might run into. Pipers can be metallers too. And why not?

*

But to get back to those who gripe…

It seems to me as though a lot of people who object to metal are actually afraid of it on some level. They'd be unlikely to say so, not in so many words, but that's the impression I get. The image, the volume and the speed of the music are simply too much to handle and are sort of intimidating.

Alternately, objections could be somewhat more earthy and based on the assumption that every band, and so potentially every fan, could wind up like a bunch of drug-addled sex-addicted Mötley Crües. What *would* the neighbours say?

There have been so many occasions on which I've heard this refrain rattle in my ears:

'Oh my God, that's shocking! Could you please just turn that *dreadful* racket down?'

To which the most effective possible response is:

'Well, no, actually. I fucking couldn't! Do you know who these guys are? Do you have any idea just how good this band really is? Do you even have a clue what you're listening to right now? No? Well, ignorance isn't bliss, believe me! What if I were to make a mad dash across the room to switch off Radio 3 just as your favourite Stravinsky concerto was beginning? How would you like that, eh?'

That normally does the trick.

In terms of volume? Yep. Metal is *supposed* to be LOUD! It's supposed to be played at high volumes on sound systems, and at gigs it's meant to be skull-piercingly thunderous. This, in itself, is often taken as just plain offensive. But that's the way it's meant to be. And in terms of the nature of the music in itself, well, it was never intended to be filed under 'easy listening'. The multifaceted nature of the music is, in fact, such a niche area to certain audiences that in some ways it could even be described as 'specialist'.

And then there's the question of lyrical subject matter. That can be a touchy issue as well, what with all those PARENTAL GUIDANCE: EXPLICIT CONTENT stickers bandied about the place. Metal lyrics vary in their own field just as much as lyrics in any other genre of music. You get the more radio-friendly stuff from some bands, and the kind of thing you need to take a shower after listening to from others. But on the other hand, if you're looking for decadent lyrics, then look no further than a lot of bands from the 1960s and 1970s. Fair enough, 'Animal (Fuck Like A Beast)' by

W.A.S.P. and 'Bastard' by Mötley Crüe were always likely to offend huge swathes of humanity, but if you look at the lyrics of 'Honkey Tonk Women' by the Stones, or 'Who Are You' by The Who, they're not exactly written for your maiden aunt either, and I think that the PMRC, if they'd been around at the time, would have had plenty to say about them. Have you ever listened to the track 'Star Star' by the Rolling Stones? Holy shit, how did they get away with that? In fact, when the Stones were asked in an interview why they had chosen the title *Some Girls* for their 1978 album, one of them, maybe Jagger, responded saying, 'Err, cuz we couldn't remember their fackin' names!' Even 'Wake Up Little Susie' by the Everly Brothers was banned for a while because its lyrics were deemed 'suggestive'.

I suppose it all depends on your personal taboo threshold.

But it goes deeper than that. A lot of detractors just assume that all metal bands sing about is devils, dragons, drinking and humping, and whilst there is a fair bit of that going on for sure, it's far from the whole picture. Iron Maiden is a case in point. From day one, their albums have been immersed in historical and literary imagery. They have written songs based on subjects such as ancient Egyptian ideas of reincarnation, the Battle of Britain, the Inquisition, Alexander the Great, and the Charge of the Light Brigade. And that's just a small sample of the historical stuff. They've also produced tracks based on classic literature such as *The Murders in the Rue Morgue* by Edgar Allan Poe, and the *Rime of the Ancient Mariner* by Samuel Taylor Coleridge. Not bad. But, further than this, bands such as Maiden, by the very nature of their lyrics, often introduce their fans to fascinating subject matter that they may never have bothered to look into before. I don't think I'd ever have read *The Loneliness of the Long-Distance Runner* or a biography of Baron Von Richthofen had it not been for Iron Maiden.

Dream Theater are worth checking out in this respect as

well. One of their earlier tracks, 'Pull Me Under', is replete with references to *Hamlet*. Metal Church's track 'Anthem to the Estranged' examines the issue of homelessness. And then there's 'Indians' by Anthrax, which looks at the way Native Americans were treated by European settlers.

So, to all the disparagers of heavy metal, please do not cross to the other side of the street. Step over here, sit down, concentrate, and listen up. Let me educate you!

AC/DC	'Heatseeker'
	'Shake Your Foundations'
Brides of Destruction	'Life'
	'Shut the Fuck Up'
Iron Maiden	'Die With Your Boots On'
Judas Priest	'Jawbreaker'
King Diamond	'Insanity'
Manowar	'Hail and Kill'
	'Warriors of the World'
Megadeth	'Hook in Mouth'
Motörhead	'Born to Raise Hell'
	'We Are the Road Crew'
W.A.S.P.	'Alive'
Wolfsbane	'Cathode Ray Clinic'
	'The Loveless'

CHAPTER 16

There are certain things that you simply do not do

Right. Good. Now that I've got that off my chest, let's pick things up again… in 1994…

I was living with a forty-five-year-old divorcee, an evangelical Christian, and a stoner. I was in shared accommodation, which was the only option Huddersfield University had on offer to a student who was in his early twenties. Two of the four burners on the oven didn't work; there was a drip in the ceiling of my room which always seemed to zero in on my pillow; and we had monstrous rodent issues.

Welcome to the world of higher education.

Having made something of a dog's breakfast of my educational career up to this point, I had inevitably needed to go through 'clearing' in order to find a university place. If I'm honest, I had foreseen that this would be likely for some time, but it was still a pain. I knew what I was interested in, but finding a course with any vacant spaces was problematic even back then. I had had amazing history teachers whilst at Mackworth College in Derby, and I wanted to follow that up. So, modern history it was to be. But exactly where I would find a course was the problem.

Eventually, after thumbing through numerous prospectuses and looking up campus locations on a road atlas, Huddersfield cropped up. An interesting-looking course, in an interesting-looking town somewhere up in Yorkshire. Okay. I called the faculty, and they invited me up to see them. Huddersfield was one of the newer universities that had only recently been upgraded from polytechnic status, and it looked pretty good to me. I was accepted as an undergraduate.

Shortly afterwards, I found myself living in a real, genuine, actual pigsty of a house with a distinctly unlikely cast of characters. The older guy, John, was there because his wife had walked in on him earlier that year whilst he was, let's say, conducting a very up close and detailed inspection of another lady's physical geography. This, understandably, resulted in a spontaneous eviction on pain of breadknife castration. The evangelical Christian, Martin, was a third-year student who kept banging on about how I needed to be '*saved*' and that my destiny was '*with the Lord!*' He kept on following me around insisting that I '*see the light*'. Yes, he was a bit creepy... And the other guy? That was Graham, with his baggy jeans and moptop haircut. I wasn't sure what his game was really. He just seemed to be mashed off his tits every single evening. And then there was me, and I happened to be there just, well, by chance really.

And the place stank!

Not that I really helped to remedy this. I was something of a slow bloomer and didn't really know all that much about housekeeping. Washing up occasionally and hoovering was fine, but anything else was something of a mystery. My meals were generally just-add-water pots of one form or another, Fray Bentos pies (usually with chips), or whatever was ready at the local takeaway. There were pizza boxes, bits of chip paper, cigarette butts, reefer roaches, and quite a lot of furry food scraps scattered hither and yon.

Hence the rodent problem.

My bedroom was on the first floor, and it served the purpose. It verified a number of typical student traits. There was an ever-growing pyramid of Tartan beer cans blocking out the light from my cracked single-glazed window; there were history books, ring binders, pieces of A4 paper with notes written on them, and other general detritus strewn around; and, naturally, there was my guitar gear: at this point a red Jackson Flying V and a Peavey amp.

I also had a gigantic *Crimson Idol* poster, showing live shots from W.A.S.P.'s slot at the Donington Monsters of Rock festival of 1992. This took pride of place.

*

Alongside the seminars, lectures, presentations and essay requirements, I needed a band. I needed to find some similarly inclined guys who wanted to dig into the seams of metal and produce some nice nuggets of gold. I could help out with that. I knew it.

So I went out looking.

I found the nearest music shops and started trawling through the 'musicians wanted' sections on their noticeboards. The adverts were pinned onto the boards and were usually written in pen. They were, however, pretty consistent: *drummer wanted, must have own kit and be committed, call this number... ; bass player needed for indie band influenced by The Smiths, Inspiral Carpets, James, etc... ; Singer needed, must be heavily into Lisa Stansfield...* See my predicament? I was a riffer and a shredder and a whammy bar diver. I was a contorted-faced soloist, who bent upwards even from the twenty-fourth fret. With me, that's what you got. And, what's more, I was actually starting to get quite good. But not in the way these indie, poppy, shoe-gazing guys were interested.

In summary, there was a plentiful lack of anything to do with metal. No adverts were referencing Maiden, Motörhead, Saxon, or even some of the more commercial stuff like Bon Jovi or Whitesnake. Nothing. Nada. I went from shop to shop, and this was the pattern: if you were into metal you were either not relevant, a dinosaur, or deemed to be crap! Some of the ads specifically stated: 'No metalheads!' I felt a bit like Tim Robbins' character at the start of *The Hudsucker Proxy* when he was shown standing eagerly outside the labour exchange waiting for a suitable job opportunity to present itself, and finding that there were in fact two options: sod all, or dead end.

This was the way things were for many aspiring metal musicians in the 1990s. We had entered the wasteland.

But, ever the optimist, I persisted.

And then one day, whilst doing my usual search, I found something that stood out. Pinned to one of the noticeboards was the advert I had been looking for. It must have been new because I would surely have noticed it before had it been more than a week old. It shouted out: WANTED: GUITARIST TO JOIN METAL BAND. MUST HAVE OWN EQUIPMENT AND BE COMMITTED.

Chuffing bleeding Nora! (As they say in Yorkshire.) That was *me!* I made a note of the contact details, double checked them, triple checked them. I bought a fresh set of Ernie Ball 9–42 gauge strings and headed back home to make the call. (Still no mobile phone yet. Yes, I was a bit of a luddite.)

I couldn't wait to get back into the swing of it. It had been a while since I'd jammed with anyone, so I was fired up and ready to go.

But when I got back home, something that I hadn't expected confronted me. There seemed to be uproar in the house. There was shouting, banging, swearing, and a clattering sound that suggested that people were being flung around all over the place! Was it a fight? Some kind of raid? Someone in there had really lost their shit about something! What was going on?

'You *bastard!*' Crash!

'You little *fucker!*' Blam!

'Over here, quick! No, here, *here!*' Clang!

Having opened the door, I did my best to interject. 'Excuse me, fellas. Erm, before I come in, what the hell is actually happening here?'

Graham spoke up: 'It's the mice, man! They're fuckin' pouring out of the bog!'

Now, I knew that this guy was partial to one or two substances but… what? Mice? Coming out of the bog?

'The bog?'

'Aye, yes, the *bog!* It's *swarming* with them!'

I hammered my way up the hall and turned right into said 'bog'.

And he was right! There was a hole in the back wall just under the U-bend. I had never paid much attention to it before. I did now though. Mice really were pouring up through it, two or three at a time.

'Oh, for crying out flaming loud!'

This was a new experience for me. An actual rodent infestation. But, given the state of the place, none of us could say we were all that surprised. This invasion had been on the cards for some time.

John was standing on the stairs, leaning over the banister and pointing out mice to Graham who was doing a good deal of scuttling around and splatting. He was using a kind of short-handled shovel, the sort of thing you might have used to scoop up dog shit before bagging became the preferred method. And he was going Rambo on these little guys!

'There's *another!*' Clomp!

There were little red splotches on the carpet and even on some of the walls, and I remember thinking to myself: this is actually… *horrific!*

But then my stomach jumped into my throat: 'They'd better not be anywhere near my axe!'

Could mice climb stairs? I was a bit vague on this one. It wasn't the sort of question I'd ever had cause to ask myself in the past, but right now it became a burning issue. What if they'd got into my room and gnawed through my guitar cables? What if this James Herbert horror scenario had conspired to scupper my first opportunity to join a metal band in Yorkshire?

I got to my room, having barged past John, who was still leaning over the banister, in about five seconds flat, and mercifully my area appeared to be clear. Thank God for that! Close one!

*

At long last, and after things had calmed down a bit, I made my phone call. I had a pen and pad handy in case I needed to take any notes. I heard the dialling tone sound a couple of times, and then the click as someone picked up.

'Hello?' said someone.

'Hi,' I said. 'Is this the guy who put up the advert in the guitar shop?'

'Yep, speaking. Who's this?'

'Oh, my name's Phil, and I'm calling about that ad. You're looking for somebody to join your band?'

Suddenly, he was all ears: 'Oh yeah, yeah, yeah! I've been looking for ages. You interested?'

'Too right I am! I've been looking for a band for months. Nobody out there seems to be interested in anything apart from Britpop and indie.'

'Yeah, I know, mate. It's shite innit? So, err, are you a guitar player then?'

'That's right.'

'Cool, we'll be needing another one of them. What kind of stuff?'

'Well, you know, Maiden, Saxon, Priest, Metallica. A bit of

Marty Friedman and things like that.' (I was exaggerating for effect, you understand? To this day, I've never been able to play a Marty Friedman solo all the way through.)

'Right. Excellent. I'm Gavin by the way. Sounds like we'd better get together. I'll give you the address of the place where we'll be jamming.'

I took it down and made sure of it. Excellent stuff. I had a time and a place and, potentially, a gig!

We got together the following week in a room behind some kind of working men's club on the outskirts of town. I'd taken the bus. It was cheaper and easier than getting a taxi, and there was a bus stop right outside the house. Having got onto and off the bus, and having shambled into the room carrying all my gear, I was met by my new bandmates, Gavin first. He was tall, hugely long-haired and blond, and he seemed to favour denim. I also noticed a large Peavey amp and a Les Paul resting in the corner. Good start. There was a big handshake and a welcome-to-the-room gesture. Then there was Paul, who was apparently a bass player. Not that he really looked the part. Crew cut, small, glasses, a bit gangly. But still, it takes all sorts to make a world, and his playing would be what mattered in the end. There was also a drum kit, but apparently no drummer as yet. He was on his way. Fair enough. If you've ever been in a band, you'll know that there's always at least one dude in the last-minute brigade. On occasion, I've been that dude myself.

Not to worry. We plugged in and tuned up. Gavin got down in front of his amp and did some fiddling around with pedals and tweaking of settings until he was content with his tone. I was more interested in volume myself. Pedals had never been my thing. My amp had enough distortion on it as it was, and that was fine with me. So we were tuned up, revved up, and ready to rock!

One, two, three, four, GO!

We jammed through 'Crazy Train', 'Paranoid', and bits of early

Metallica. Gavin had a *Hmm, this appears to have some potential* expression on his face, at least when I could see it. His hair was swinging around like a Dutch windmill. Paul continued in his expressionless manner. It was almost as though he was wearing a wooden mask. On the other hand, however, his playing was absolutely flipping unbelievable! We weren't jamming rocket science music, but he was approaching it in a rocket science way. Was this some kind of child prodigy? Was he prog rock's unspoken and unknown secret weapon? I could be chugging along on a nice easy E chord, and he would be jamming some exotic scale up near his twelfth fret. In short, he was shredding out lead bass! But he appeared to be completely unmoved by this astonishing gift that he had.

And then the door to the room cracked open. Could this be a drummer? We strangled our strings and wound down the volume knobs.

'All right guys?' said the new someone.

'Hey, Steve, come on in,' said Gavin. 'Meet Phil. Phil, this is Steve. Steve, Phil. Phil's auditioning tonight.'

'All right, Phil? How's it going mate? I'm Steve.'

Having established 'Steve', Gavin, Paul and I carried on, two guitars and bass, whilst he fiddled with his sticks, adjusted the drum stool, and nodded to the groove.

He joined in. WHUP, *BAP,* WHUP, *BAP,* WHUP, *BAP, CRAASSSHH!* He sounded solid enough. AC/DC covers would probably be fine with him.

So, AC/DC it was. We went for 'Back in Black' and 'Highway to Hell'. Yeah, this was sounding good. It was definitely recognisable, and basically all the parts were there. Except for the vocals. Apparently, no vocalist had been in touch to say that they were interested in jamming. For the time being this was okay though. We were on the right track and playing the sort of music we wanted to hear.

I chucked in a few solos here and there, and so did Gavin. He turned out to be a huge Extreme fan, and was big on Nuno Bettencourt. Impressive indeed, although I was more of a Kerry King man myself.

We carried on like this for about an hour and a half before we decided to call it an evening. Everyone seemed to approve of what I could do. Even Paul appeared to raise his eyebrows in approval from time to time, although this may have been my imagination.

At the end of the session we packed up our gear. The other three got together in a huddle over in one of the corners. They were whispering together, looking over at me, and then whispering some more. You know when you're being talked about, don't you?

Gavin stepped up to me. 'Okay, mate, if you want it, you're in!'

This was hardly a discussion point from where I was standing. Of *course* I wanted it! *Damn right* I wanted it! Hands were shaken all round and thumbs up signs were made.

I was in! I was signed up as the new member of... well, the band didn't actually have a name yet, but I was in anyway, and that was all that mattered to me. And these guys were actually all right. There was potential here.

The following week we got back together, same time same place. This was going to be a fantastic follow-up to the audition session. To start with, everyone was on time, so after warming up and flexing our fingers with a bluesy jam, we started to discuss what we actually wanted to play and how we were going to play it.

And that was when things started to head a bit southward.

In short, Gavin wanted to move with the times. I didn't. I was absolutely rooted in the 1980s and, on a practical basis, thrash metal. Thrash was not Gavin's favourite flavour. In fact, he couldn't stand it. It didn't take much to read this in his facial expressions whenever I was hammering away on the E string and pulling San Francisco Bay Area riffs out of my red Jackson. That cat-with-brain-freeze expression doesn't leave much to the imagination. He spent quite a lot of time watching my fingers flying around on my fretboard, and my picking hand, and doing his best to follow what I was playing.

Meanwhile, he would be hitting big chords and riffs in the style of the Wildhearts or Korn. Okay, but that wasn't what *I* wanted to be playing. He also had a liking for effects pedals which just seemed to make the weirdest sounds. Was I interested in experimenting with this kind of thing? No, not really. A lot of volume and distortion was the key to metal as far as I was concerned. And I was absolutely certain that I was correct on that score.

Musical differences? Yep, that old chestnut!

But not to worry, maybe we could find our way around this. Who could say?

Then Gavin piped up: 'Hey, Phil, how do you fancy trying out a bit of vocals? You said you'd done a bit before?'

Had I? I could have. I had, very briefly, sung in a metal band whilst at college. My pal Richard had played lead in that band. He was some guitar player. God, he could shred! Had I mentioned my vocal experimentations in our phone conversation a couple of weeks ago? Presumably.

'Me? Erm, well, yes but only a bit, and that was way back. But yeah, okay. I'll… give it a go. Is that mike over there plugged in?'

'Yeah, we got it all set up before you arrived.'

So that's why they were all there on time was it?

And the track that Gavin suggested was 'Livin' on the Edge' by Aerosmith. *What?* I could handle Steve Earle or some Stones' tracks vocally, but my ability to rasp out a Steven Tyler impression commanded pretty lengthy odds.

And then there was the problem of playing and singing at the same time. Had strumming been all that was required, then no problem. But this was a particularly twiddly Aerosmith number. A different ball game altogether.

I gave it a shot.

Oh deary, deary me. So much for melody. It sounded more like I was peeling a weasel!

The hand-waving head-shaking consensus made its way around the room in double quick time. It was requested unanimously that I, for pity's sake, cease and desist!

I thought this dismal performance may have been enough to get me off the hook, but apparently this was not the case. Unbelievably, Gavin suggested that, by way of alternative, I try 'Paradise City' by G N' R instead. I was just recovering from having demonstrated my innate inability to imitate Stephen Tyler, and now he wanted me to impersonate Axl Rose? Dream on, buddy! This was not likely to happen, especially if, once again, I had to play one of the guitar parts. I must have had a noncommittal expression on my face, because when I looked over in Gavin's direction, he lowered his eyes and looked at his shoes for a moment. He then gave me an encouraging nod to suggest that trying this track might actually be a good idea.

Well, all right then. If you're going to dive in, you might as well go for the belly-flop! Take a deep breath, Phil, you're going to need a lung-full in order to have any *prayer* of nailing this one.

But then there was another problem: Steve. He had also been looking at Gavin and expressing a slightly uncomfortable demeanour. What was going on now? Did he need a piss or something? I'm sure that was permitted, and that he didn't need to put his hand up and call out, 'Sir, sir, please, sir, I need to go to the toilet, sir!' Oh well, whatever. I thought it best to just crash on through this new request and ignore him for the time being.

Gavin started the intro, but then Steve shouted out, 'Hang on, guys, I'm not sure if I know this one.' We all stopped what we were doing and looked at him. Didn't know this one? How could that possibly be? It was almost like saying that he didn't know the tune to 'Happy Birthday'! This single by Guns N' Roses was massive, and part of the life-blood of the up-to-date rock fan. I mean, it was played and heard everywhere. Honestly, which planet had this guy been living on? It certainly couldn't have been a local one. Even my mum knew 'Paradise City', and she wasn't what you might call a Gunners fan! 'Paradise City' was one of the most famous tracks in the world back then. And Steve was a *rock drummer*? How was it even feasible that this track had passed him by? Oh shit!

And then a cardinal sin was committed. Gavin appeared to have an idea. 'Hey, Steve, mate. Let me show you. It's real easy. Give me your sticks for a sec.'

Oh shit, indeed!

Now let's be clear about this. A non-drummer does not go into a rehearsal room and show a drummer how to play drums. This does not need to be codified in statute; it's an unwritten understanding. There are certain things that you simply *do not do*. If there had been an Eleventh Commandment chiselled onto Moses's tablets upon his descent from Mount Sinai, it could quite reasonably have read: THOU SHALT NOT COVET THY DRUMMER'S STICKS'.

Steve's expression changed from slightly concerned to red-faced and dangerously pissed off in the time it took to blink! He got up from his drum stool and rose to a surprising height. Gavin seemed to shrink in proportion and froze midstride.

'You lay a *finger* on my sticks and you'll be shitting splinters till Christmas, pal! Am I making myself clear?'

He was. Gavin backed right off.

He then tried to gain back a little ground: 'Er, sorry, mate. I didn't mean to... Well, you know, I thought that if I...'

'Yeah, yeah. I know what you thought, you little prick. Shove it up your arse! Find yourselves another drummer! Get fucked, the lot of you!'

And that was that. Steve was gone, and we just stood there looking at the door as the cloud of dust gradually subsided.

I, for one, never saw him again. As for the others, who knows? After that rehearsal I never saw any of them again either.

Chuffing Nora! So much for that.

Aerosmith	'Big Ten Inch Record'
	'Kings and Queens'
Black Sabbath	'Nightwing'
Guns N' Roses	'Since I Don't Have You'
Morbid Angel	'Sworn to the Black'
Motörhead	'Shoot You in the Back'
	'The Ace of Spades'
Ozzy	'I Just Want You'
	'No More Tears'
Paradise Lost	'As I Die'
Soul Asylum	'Runaway Train'
	'Somebody to Shove'
Stiltskin	'Inside'
Warlock	'I Rule the Ruins'
Yngwie Malmsteen	'Seventh Sign'

CHAPTER 17

Tempus fugit

It was 1997. I was living in Manchester. And I was 'avin' it LAAAARRRGGGE!

Manchester, at that time, was probably one of the most happening cities in the world. Everything seemed to be going on there at the same time. Manchester United were repeatedly obliterating just about every other top-flight team in the English Premiership and in Europe; the club scene, and the rave scene in particular, was becoming massive; Oasis were at the point of releasing their third album, which was set to become a huge global seller; and redevelopments of formerly run-down parts of the city were in full flow. Manchester was ALIVE!

However, my principal reason for being in Manchester was actually none of these things. I had gone there in order to study for a master's degree in Modern European History, and I was planning on being in the city for about a year. Additionally, Andrew had done his Law degree in Manchester a few years earlier and was still living there. So there was a family connection too. All was good in the hood.

Manchester also had an amazing attribute that would have appealed to metalheads of just about any persuasion. This attribute was a club called Jilly's Rockworld. And rock it certainly did! You entered Jilly's through a plain and nondescript door on Oxford Road, then made your way down the stairs into the dark corridors below. You knew you were going the right way because you could hear the shrieking sounds of guitars getting louder and louder as you went. And then the room opened up and you were there. In the mecca of Manchester's metal scene. Manchester wasn't entirely about bands like the Charlatans, James, and the Smiths. As this club showed, there was a considerable amount of metal in Mancunian blood as well.

Jilly's was sweaty, smoky and jam-packed on every occasion I was there. It was also as hot as hell. I don't think the management bothered all that much with the air conditioning.

This club covered all the bases. It didn't matter what you were into. If you wanted to hear Slayer, you just needed to go and let the DJ know. And the same went for just about anything else the discerning metalhead might have wanted to hear. They played Alice Cooper, Metallica, Maiden, Skid Row, Anthrax, Ozzy… you name it. And everyone was right into it. On Friday nights the place was always jumping.

Of course, there was no dress code in the way there would have been in the trendy clubs. At Jilly's anything went. You would usually see folk kitted out in leather, lace, latex, rubber and just about anything else. There would be long-hairs, mohawks, dreadlocks, and folk with hair bleached just about every colour under the sun. Very cool. I was usually of the denim persuasion myself, but you saw some sights in there and no mistake!

And they shredded out metal. And I mean shredded! The volume in there was immense. I'm sure it would have made even Lemmy proud. Health and Safety would probably have something to say about it these days, but, well, you know, whatever…

Also, Jilly's stayed open all night. Whilst most clubs were turfing people out at about 2am, Jilly's just kept on cranking it. I was down there with Andrew and some of his pals one night, and at about two in the morning they just switched DJs. One shift ended and another started. And what a start it was. The new guy kicked off his set with the title track from Ice T's *Body Count* album. I went berserk! Full-on power stance with air guitar raging, and meticulous attention paid to all the chord changes. My hair was blasting back and forth as though I was in an Icelandic gale, and I was bellowing out every lyric, not that I could hear myself of course. Much more and I could well have become a soft tissue whiplash case in the Manchester Royal Infirmary, but I was made of tougher stuff than that.

And what's more, amazingly, Jilly's Rockworld served breakfast! Well, breakfast of a sort. If you were one of those customers who just had to push on through till dawn, then your needs would be catered for. At around seven o'clock in the morning, if you so desired, you could purchase from behind the bar – wait for it – a Pot Noodle! Now, can you honestly think of another nightclub that did anything like that?

*

There was also something interesting going on in the W.A.S.P. camp.

There had been rumours floating around that Chris Holmes was back in the band. Just rumours and nothing more. But still, the possibility of a reunion with Blackie Lawless was tantalising enough for me. The last time they had recorded together, they'd thrown down the extraordinary *Headless Children* album.

~~~Cut to 1989~~~

I had lived and died by W.A.S.P.'s *Headless Children* album whilst I was in the sixth form at school. Where metal was concerned, this was magnetic north. It hit so hard it could have caused seismic activity in the earth's crust. You would need to be careful if you were ever planning on playing this album anywhere near the San Andreas Fault! Just hit play on 'The Heretic (The Lost Child)', or 'The Neutron Bomber' and you'll see exactly what I'm talking about! The riffs, the lyrics, the solos?

Talk about hitting the spot!

And it hadn't just been the amazing tracks that were on this release. The album cover art was bizarre, and, incidentally, guaranteed to put the PMRC's backs up. Which may in fact have been the point! It wasn't a picture of the band, or, as was the case on most occasions, just of Blackie by himself. It appeared, on first glance, to simply show a jumble of folk standing in front of a huge gaping skull which dominated the background. However, closer scrutiny belied this. Right up front, and blatantly visible, you could see an image of Jack Ruby shooting Lee Harvey Oswald; Joseph Stalin was shown grinning in from the left-hand side; there was a blank-faced Adolf Hitler looking out at the viewer; there were KKK members; and even Idi Amin was shown... amongst others! What in merry hell was going on here?[5]

I remember seeing *The Headless Children* in a little independent music shop in Derby called R. E. Cords shortly after its release. Obviously, this album needed to be bought. There was no question about that. Over to the cassette racks, pick it up, take it to the till, and pay the man!

---

5   Whilst studying in Manchester, I looked into World War Two propaganda cartoons. One particular image struck me. It was produced in 1942, and was entitled 'The Gate of Stalingrad'. It immediately reminded me of W.A.S.P.'s *Headless Children* album cover. Could this image have been the basis for the album's artwork?

Having got it back home, I ensconced myself in my room and read through the lyrics meticulously. Having done so, I took another look at them and did a bit of head scratching. This certainly wasn't what I'd been expecting. Were these honestly Blackie's lyrics?

War?

Politics?

Death and bereavement?

Where, I asked myself, were the tracks about humping, drinking, and tripping until you were twatted off your noggin? I trapped the tape in my cassette deck and braced myself. What followed was about fifty minutes of the most amazing, staggering metal! I sat there staring at the stereo with my eyes on stalks! Track after track simply seared through the speakers. Chris's solos were blistering, and Blackie's voice was stronger than I'd ever heard it. I found myself thinking, 'How the hell has a band like W.A.S.P. managed to produce an album like this? My God, they've taken every brilliant part of what they've done in the past and put them all together right here. This is mind-blowing!'

It was a major cut above what the band had produced before both musically and lyrically. As you'll have gathered, I liked it.

~~~ Cut back to 1997: the HMV shop, Market Street, Manchester ~~~

Now, in my mind, this set the scene nicely for a new W.A.S.P. album. In this climate of post-grunge, miserable, slit-your-wrists rock, an injection of old-fashioned rock 'n' roll tunes by Messrs Lawless and Holmes would be just the tonic. There were a couple of other guys in the band now, but membership of W.A.S.P. had been a revolving door scenario since its inception, so this was hardly anything new. What mattered was that the core of the band had been re-established. This was huge!

However.

And it was quite a big however.

I picked the newly released W.A.S.P. CD up off the rack. The album cover was a bit questionable. It wasn't all that clear what it was even depicting. It appeared to show a kind of grainy sepia image of a closed fridge in a dark cellar room. Errmm… righty ho. The band's logo was shown across the middle, and some smudged faded writing was tucked in beneath it. Strange. Were there hidden meanings to be found here? W.A.S.P. wasn't known for being a subliminal band, that's for sure.

I took a closer look. Then, on its spine, I saw three initials: *K.F.D.* Okay. But still in the dark with this.

I flipped the disc over to check out the track listing, and there it was: track one, 'Kill Fuck Die'!

'…?'

There was, unsurprisingly, a 'PARENTAL GUIDANCE: EXPLICIT CONTENT' sticker on the front of the album. Well now, that was a piece of deductive genius which fell squarely into the 'no-shit-Sherlock' category of the glaringly obvious!

Naturally, my mind had imposed a compulsory purchase order on this album, but I had my guard up. I felt that this might be a little different to what I had been expecting. And bugger me with a broom handle if I wasn't right!

Were those keyboards, or some kind of strange overly distorted guitars? Was that a drum machine? Did the guy in the shop accidentally slip a Nine Inch Nails album into the CD case? (No disrespect, Mr Reznor. NIN's just not my bag, that's all.) What the hell was I listening to? This certainly did not hark back to the glory days of the 1980s. If anything, the whole sound, taking into account who was in the band, was just plain confusing. This was, basically, very heavy industrial metal, and that flew in the face of everything W.A.S.P. stood for. I sat at my desk and listened to the album all the way through, puzzled. All I could think was, 'What are they playing at? How can one of my favourite bands have come out with *this*? Maybe, one day, possibly, it might grow on me. But maybe not, eh?'

It just goes to show that sometimes the unexpected belts you one right between the eyes and you find yourself stunned for the wrong reasons. *K.F.D.* was, what might be called, a 'challenging' album. A lot of bands put out albums from time to time which leave you wondering, 'What are these guys thinking?' That was definitely what had happened here!

I stuck with it though. As a fan, that's what you do. I did find a standout track entitled 'My Tortured Eyes'. And, weirdly, it was the ballad. If it could be called a ballad. It certainly wasn't lovey-dovey stuff, but it did have a great eerie feel to it, and a hoofing solo by Holmes.

But tellingly, all of the tracks from this album have been dropped from W.A.S.P.'s live sets, and it's pretty clear why. W.A.S.P. is all about 'Wild Child', 'Blind in Texas', 'Chainsaw Charlie', 'On Your Knees', and 'L.O.V.E. Machine'. Now that's where it's really at!

Having said that, there was one occasion upon which the *K.F.D.* album really did come into its own. It was one of those unplanned things that really shouldn't have happened at all. I was in Manchester University's library doing some late-night research for an essay. As was my wont in those days, I had my CD Walkman on and was cranking the album into my brain. I was persevering with it and had just got to the final track: 'The Horror'. Now, if you're familiar with this track, fine. You'll understand that the lyrics are on the fairly strong side. If you're not, for crying out loud approach it with caution. It is likely to leave a lasting impression and possibly psychological scars. This one makes Marilyn Manson sound like Tammy Wynette!

You know when you're listening to music on headphones and you start speaking, the volume of your voice tends to rise relative to the volume of what you're hearing? Yes? Well, that's exactly what was happening to me whilst I was listening to this track. I was sitting at one of the tables with a stack of books and a notepad in front of me. I had my head down, and I was grafting. And just then it must have started. The infernal and repeated refrain at the end of 'The Horror' kicked in, and I kicked right in with it. The thing is, I had no idea how loudly I was belting it out. As far as I was concerned, I was just mumbling it under my breath so as not to cause any kind of disturbance. Evidently, this wasn't the case. But I sort of got away with it. Rather than being told to 'Get the hell out of here, you *fucking maniac*', a bloke stuck his head out from the end of one of the book stacks close to where I was working and stared at me with a motionless expression on his face. Right then, I realised what had happened, and I started to scramble up some kind of spontaneous apology to offer this guy. I don't think it would have cut much ice, but, as it happened, it wouldn't have mattered. When he managed to get hold of his voice, his first words were: 'Dude, that was *AWESOME!*' A kindred spirit. That was a bit of luck. God knows what would have happened if it had been a lecturer or a librarian up there instead. The bloke in the library turned out to be a huge metal fan and he was practically desperate to find out what I was listening to. We headed down to the students' union bar, talked metal till we got chucked out, and ended up mortally wasted!

*

But 1997 was not all about questionable musical directions. There was nothing questionable about what Megadeth was getting up to. They were as solid as a rock and were holding down the best line-up they'd ever had. The *Clash of the Titans* personnel were still in place, and they were still delivering. Mustaine and Friedman's playing on their new album, *Cryptic Writings*, was top notch.

They were playing a gig in Manchester, and Richard and I decided that we needed to be there. You don't just pass a Megadeth gig by, not if you're a true metal fan. That would be tantamount to heresy! We got hold of tickets as soon as they were available, and on the night we made sure we were close to the front of the queue.

As we were loitering around by the main gates waiting to be allowed in, I took a slightly closer look at the queue. Something about this queue looked a little different, but I couldn't quite put my finger on it. The T-shirts were all in order, and the banter was just the same as always. But then it struck me: there were, noticeably, quite a few bald heads, pot bellies and grey beards shuffling along in the line. It wasn't just a long column of hairy yoof any more. Time was visibly starting to catch up with us. It was pointless trying to deny it: we were closer to the millennium than to 1985. No two ways – *tempus fugit!*

As it was, neither Richard nor I had any interest in Old Father Time. Our main concern was getting a good spot near the stage barrier. And with a bit of elbowing and muscling through the rapidly developing audience, we did.

We were much closer than when I had seen Megadeth at the Birmingham NEC seven years earlier. And to be close to the barrier at a gig such as this was quite something in itself. Especially as we had manoeuvred ourselves to Marty Friedman's side of the stage. As guitar players, we needed to watch this guy closely. This was likely to be a masterclass.

After a slightly strange support slot (this was 1997 and some seriously weird shit was going down in the music business), we were both, alongside a few thousand others, set for a huge night of authentic balls-to-the-wall metal.

And then, lights down, and WHACK! They were on! 'Holy Wars: The Punishment Due'. What a kick-off! Mr Friedman was literally about six feet away from us, and he was pouring out the riffs in his usual smooth and effortless manner. How the hell could he play like that? He made it look so damn easy. And Mr Mustaine was to his right, snarling into the mike and chugging away on his silver Flying V.

This was a good night to be a metal fan!

Megadeth's wicked magic was certainly still there. There was no posing or fakery on stage, and as for grunge, Megadeth shattered it into splinters! Stalwart tracks such as 'Wake Up Dead', 'Sweating Bullets', and 'Hanger 18' were all thrown in, and the band sounded better in this smaller venue than they had in the huge and cavernous NEC. They also incorporated numerous newer tracks such as 'A Secret Place' and 'Trust'. But when they played 'She Wolf' I just about lost it! I've always been a sucker for harmonised guitar solos, and the one at the end of this track was the highlight of their new album. And to be able to watch it being played from so close to the stage. Mesmerised? Yes, mesmerised!

Final encore?

'Anarchy in the UK'.

Naturally.

When Mustaine stepped up to the mike for this one, he looked savage-eyed and just plain dangerous. He looked sufficiently keyed up as to rip someone's head off! And Friedman came on holding this bizarre-looking guitar. It wasn't really a Flying V, it was too curved and stretched out for that. It had crop-circle inlays on its neck and looked like it was coated in a kind of silver film. (A Jackson Roswell Rhoads, Richard sagely informed me.) As the band charged through their final bludgeoning attack, I spent the entire time checking out this amazing-looking guitar.

Megadeth's set ripped the venue to pieces! Their attack on stage was still incredible, and I remember briefly thinking about all those shoe-gazing Manchester bands from the indie scene. Maybe they could have taken a few pages out of Megadeth's how-to-blow-an-audience-away manual.

Aerosmith	'Pink'
Black Sabbath	'Snowblind'
	'The Writ'
Body Count	'Body Count'
Gamma Ray	'One with the World'
	'Beyond the Black Hole'
Marty Friedman	'Valley of Eternity'
Megadeth	'Almost Honest'
	'Secret Place'
Metallica	'Hero of the Day'
	'Until It Sleeps'
Thunder	'Dirty Love'
	'An Englishman on Holiday'
W.A.S.P.	'My Tortured Eyes'
Yngwie Malmsteen	'Overture 1622'

CHAPTER 18

Out with the old,
in with the new

I really didn't know how much more of this I could take. It was
chewing away at me, day and night, and I honestly couldn't empty
my mind of it. I'd hit a wall. A major one. And I felt completely
encircled. I simply couldn't batter my way through to the clear air
and freedom on the other side. So, rather than trying to scale it,
I dug. How low could I go? Thinking about it now, probably not
much deeper, not much at all.

Yes, depression is a dreadful, dreadful thing, so I won't dwell
on it for too long. It's enough to say that it was all part of the path,
and that it had a habit of raising its red-eyed fang-licking face
from time to time. But at the age of twenty-nine, this creature
was crushing the very spirit out of me. It troubled me during
the daytime and haunted my dreams at night. It left me feeling
like a dried-up valueless husk – picked clean and worthless;
in short, a pointless waste of space. I was just trudging, head
down, into pummelling storms over and over again. I couldn't
see an escape route. And no quantity of counsellors with their
steepled fingers, understanding looks and slightly greying

empathy-beards were making any damned difference. My head was buggered!

As the new millennium began, I found myself sitting in an office in Nottingham, usually with my face resting on my right palm and a phone receiver pressed up against my left ear. The job basically involved being deskbound in front of a computer and responding to complaints letters which customers of this company (mentioning no names) had written, scrawled, or maybe even crayoned onto whatever they could cram into an envelope. I was required to phone said customers, sometimes purely in order to help me decipher what they had written, and this usually involved getting screamed at. The role was mentally deadening, and in my ever-aching head it felt like I was trapped in a pitch-black dungeon. So much for all that grafting at university! Should I have bothered studying at all? All that endeavour seemed to be completely needless in the real, working world. And as for my long-standing ambition to play lead guitar in a metal band? That had gone to hell in a handcart! On my daily commute from Derby, I got into the habit of playing Yngwie Malmsteen's 'End of My Rope' on an ever-repeating loop, whilst steering with one finger and paying hardly any attention to the motorway traffic.

Yes, I was a bit messed up back then.

The only real appeal of the job was Friday nights. A crowd of staff would head out into Nottingham and get leathered by pub-crawling the various happy hours which dropped the prices of shots down to something like students' union levels. Predictably, with about fifteen of us all fixing to get tanked, things usually got messy very quickly. A colleague of mine (let's call her Karen for the sake of discretion) embraced all of this to the full. Karen was what might be described as the office 'character'. She was big, bubbly and full of bounce. And, wow, did she know how to party! Additionally, she was quite happy to tell everybody about what she had got up to, and, quite often, what had got up her, during her adventures.

I slunk into work one Monday morning with all the enthusiasm of finding that I had been selected to be next in the guillotine experiment trials, and there was Karen, beaming, in the corner.

'Morning,' I probably wheezed as I sat down at my computer and tried to remember how to log onto it.

'Hiya!' she in all likelihood chimed, having got herself all set up and ready for the day.

'All right?'

'Yeah! Had a wicked time last Friday night!'

'Mmm?' (What the hell was my password?)

'Got wankered!' She loved that word. She used it a lot. 'And I pulled!'

'Oh, really? That's very interesting...'

'Yeah! There was this bloke who came up to me and asked me for a fag. So I gave him one, and then he took me outside, shoved me up against a wall and snogged me! I like the kind of bloke who'll do that. Assertive, you know?'

'Erm. Wha...?'

'He was dead classy too. He even brought his own johnnies!'

I spat my early morning coffee, and the manager, who was easily within earshot, lifted his head and looked across the room with a gaping *What the fuck did I just hear?* expression on his face. Then, upon realising that it was only Karen and that this was quite normal, he settled back to his routine.

Karen continued to beam.

Every office needs a Karen. It's that kind of craziness that keeps you sane. Let's raise a glass to all the Karens of the world!

*

But what I needed was a change, root and branch. I was burned out and dead-eyed. There was no way I could stay static in a role which was so psychologically suffocating. I needed to freshen up my mind: out with the old, in with the new. We've probably all been there at some point in our lives.

And then, from out of the blue (in fact, via an overheard conversation at an adjacent pub table somewhere in Derby), the idea of teaching English abroad came up. I'd dabbled with the idea in the past, but I'd never taken it all that seriously. Honestly, was I the sort of person who would do something like that?

Apparently, I was.

I went up to Pitlochry in Scotland to do the teaching course, and, having passed it, started looking for places to go with my new-found qualification. Maybe Spain, possibly Italy, how about Portugal? There were quite a few openings in each of these countries. But then someone pointed out that Poland was crying out for English language teachers, and why didn't I try looking for a school over there? Why not indeed? I'd hardly ever been abroad at that point in my life, so just about anything outside of the UK would be new to me. And to be on the far side of the Iron Curtain line sounded interesting and kind of mysterious. This really would be a change of backdrop.

I spent two years in Poland.

During my first year there, I taught schoolkids in a little town called Ostrów Mazowiecka, which is in the north-east of the country, close to the Masurian Lakes. I was the only native English speaker in the town. This made even the simplest of things tricky: ordering a beer; asking directions to somewhere; even explaining to a taxi driver where I lived! When I went to a café or a restaurant, I started off by just ordering whatever I could pronounce: I'd find out what it was when it arrived and gradually piece things together. To begin with, when I could speak only a few words of Polish (*tak*, *nie*, and *nie viem*), I took an English/Polish dictionary and a small pocket-sized local map with me whenever I went into town, just in case. You had to think of things like that. There was no Google Translate in 2001.

Having arrived in Poland, I was presented with a pleasant surprise: metal music was a huge deal over there. Whereas grunge and Britpop were all the rage in the UK, in Poland you could freely see long-hairs wearing Ozzy, Metallica, and Megadeth T-shirts all over the place. Old-school metal bands were completely hip! And, naturally, the Scorpions were massive. That track 'Wind of Change' could be heard everwhere. I suppose there was a good reason for that.

I bought a small portable stereo which had a cassette deck and a CD player. I used it to tune in to any radio stations I could find that had decent reception. The music ones were always preferable as Polish conversation completely baffled me. I would just have it on as background much of the time, but one evening, whilst I was perched on my sofa planning the following day's lessons, I heard out of the corner of my ear the words 'metal', 'old-school' and 'W.A.S.P.'!

WHAT?

All thoughts of tomorrow's lessons dissolved, and my attention became rivetted to this DJ. I turned up the volume. Screw the neighbours, this was important! The DJ went on in Polish for a while, but that was okay. I'd understood what I had needed to hear. And then it started. It was a new track, not some old classic, which, although always welcome, could usually be quite predictable. This was fresh and raw!

Straight for the throat! Blackie and the boys smashed into it, hell for leather. The riffing was fast, tight, and it hit like a knuckleduster! There was real energy here all right. The DJ had been dead on the money when he'd mentioned 'old-school'. This track had it in spades. It immediately had me scrunching up my nose, sticking my chin out, and nodding my head. The lyrics were all to do with darkness, questions about religion, and coiled serpents. Blackie was on form. Then the solo flooded out of the speakers, and it complemented the track perfectly. God, this was good stuff! But what was I actually hearing? I needed, at least, to know the name of this track. I wouldn't be able to phone in and request that it be played again. The DJ came back on the air.

I listened for anything that I might be able to understand...

Something, something, something, 'old-school' something, 'W.A.S.P.', something, something, '"My Wicked Heart"'. Wow! Eu-fucking-reka! Even the title was awesome!

Then it struck me that this was a mainstream radio station. I've no idea which one, but it was maybe the equivalent of Radio 2 in the UK. And they had just played a new track by W.A.S.P.? This would never have happened in Britain. And I mean never! Can you imagine Zoe Ball running through her Breakfast Show and, from out of the blue, dropping a W.A.S.P. number? Nope, neither can I. But it would be brilliant if she did though. Maybe I should send in a request, you know, just to test the water...

But as for that Polish DJ, whoever it may have been, *dziękuję*, mate! You played a blinder!

*

Whilst living in Ostrów, I didn't have all that much to do in the evenings. Let's face it, when you're the only English speaker in a small backwater town, the only people you can reasonably interact with on a conversational basis are school-age kids, and the phone lines and internet connections are hit and miss at best, options are somewhat limited. But I did have a TV. A window onto the world. It was an old Russian set, and you sometimes had to clobber the side of it in order to get the picture to hold, but it wasn't bad. Again, I tuned in to whatever I could make the most sense of. *Polsat*, one of the biggest channels over there, was easy to get hold of, but practically impossible to understand. I persisted, however, often just by staring at the screen. But there were music channels and, like with the radio, highly metallic curveballs were sometimes slung at you with no warning.

Once again, I was sitting in my flat minding my own business and probably sinking a couple of Lech or Okocim beers, when the mood of the music channel switched from pop/disco/rap/other things that just go directly over my head, to something that drilled its way right into my cranium. Whatever this was, it was dark, heavy and absolutely ironclad!

Better pay attention to this.

The video was shot partially in black and white and partially in colour, and it was from a band I didn't recognise. The guys in the band were clearly very young, so this could have been a new group, maybe a local one. There was a lot of dense forest imagery, and the video showed a man in a cape who was running around with a scythe. Now, what was going on here? The music had a strange freshness and brightness to it, but at the same time it was as dark as hell. It was brutally heavy and yet disarmingly melodic all the way through. There was a liquid fluency to the guitar playing which I hadn't heard in a metal band for a while. There were also very delicate keyboard sounds which broke through from time to time. And then... oh yeah, now that's what I call a guitar solo!

Okay, you've got me.

I grabbed a pen and paper. I always kept something to write with handy whilst watching music channels, just in case a track came on by a band I'd never heard of that had a Polish name I couldn't pronounce. Who *were* these guys? I got up close to the screen, pen poised, and waited for the caption to come up. Words appeared at the bottom of the screen: Children of Bodom, with their track 'Everytime I Die'.

Never heard of them.

But, man, got to hear that one again!

My mission now was pretty damn obvious: to find the album that featured this track, and this would involve a bus trip into Warsaw. Remember, there was no internet connection for downloading, and no Amazon.com option either. I would have to go out and do some legwork on an old-fashioned physical search.

And that was a good thing because I loved Warsaw. That weekend, I headed down to Ostrów's bus station and, having scrummed my way onto the bus, sat down to enjoy the trip. The route ran south-west through some of Poland's dense woodlands, and I just relaxed and admired the view. The journey only took about an hour.

I arrived at Warsaw bus station and made my way through to the city centre on foot. It was easy enough to find even without a map. Slap bang in the middle of Warsaw was a building which dwarfed all the others. It was a massive grey monolith with vertical sides, and it completely dominated the skyline. On a clear day, it could be seen from way outside the city's boundaries, and for many years there was a law that no other building could be constructed in Warsaw above a certain height so as to ensure its enduring domination. This building, which was constructed in the 1950s, was called the Palace of Culture and Science. It was said to be a 'gift' from Stalin to the people of Poland. Some benefactor!

On one of Warsaw's main shopping streets, Marshalkowska, there was a branch of a chain store called Empik. Empik had branches all around the country, but this one was probably the biggest. You could buy books, clothes, posters and magazines, but what I was after was the music section. The main entrance to Empik was directly across the road from the Palace, and, ironically, just a couple of hundred yards away from an icon of American culture: an enormous branch of McDonald's. East meets West *in extremis!*

I was after cassettes. CDs were widely available in Poland but, even for the same album, they were usually about twice the price. Why? No idea. Hence cassettes. There was a huge selection in Empik, and just about everything was covered. There was Polish chart music, masses of folk and classical albums, pop, disco, and of course all the big Western bands were featured. But, me being me, I was after the metal section, and, lo and behold, there it was stretching out before me. I had a feeling that I would do well here.

I started flicking through the racks in time honoured fashion… and…. yes! Children of Bodom. Found it! I picked out the cassette and flipped it over. Track one, two, three, and there it was: track four, 'Everytime I Die'. The album itself was called *Follow the Reaper*. Ahh. Now the guy with the scythe made sense.

Sold.

And it turned out that they weren't Polish; they were from Finland. Well, fair enough.

But I wasn't done yet. Maybe if I did a bit more browsing, and I had plenty of time seeing as the day was still young, I might find a few more interesting slabs of steel. I'd heard that there was a Polish band called Vader. They were a death metal group which had started up in the 1980s, at about the same time the likes of Morbid Angel and Possessed had got underway in America. I had been going through a bit of a dry spell death metal wise, so I thought I'd seek them out. And, as if by magic, ta daa! – Vader by the truckload! I didn't want to buy everything they had ever released, but judging by the number of their albums available in Empik, it could have been an option. I'd never heard them, so I thought I'd take a punt on their *Revelations* album. Excellent. And onwards. Now, what was this? It certainly looked different. The cover art showed a woman in a white dress kneeling in front of a waterfall. It looked like the kind of fantasy image which could have come from a graphic novel. The band? Nightwish, with an album called *Century Child*. Again, this was uncharted territory, but it looked interesting. Maybe I would give this one a try too, because you never know. And they came from Finland as well. What a rocking country!

So, all in all, I had a very productive day in Warsaw. Shopping in Empik was just like shopping at Way Ahead Records, but with slightly better lighting. I'd been able to pick up albums by three bands that I didn't even know. And, naturally, I had my Walkman with me, so I could start ramming them home immediately. I crossed the road, shunted up to the viewing gallery of the Palace of Culture and Science, and began. Take that, Stalin!

*

Summers in Poland are steaming hot. There is a popularly held misconception in the West that Poland is an inherently cold country, and that everything over there is perpetually stricken with permafrost. Well, okay then, at times the winters are, literally, Baltic! The rivers, and I mean the big ones, the Vistula and the Bug, often freeze right the way across for weeks at a time. The lakes in Masuria go rock solid, and the ground turns into frosted granite. No doubt about it, if you're heading over to Poland for a winter holiday, take it from me, you'll need to pack your thermals! One morning during my second year in Poland, whilst I was living in Warsaw, I remember heading out to teach at an office right on the fringes of the city. It had snowed solidly during the night, and the sun had barely risen. As I crunched through the shin-high snow, I could feel my body starting to seize up. Fortunately, I didn't have to walk all that far from the tram stop, only a couple of hundred yards, but when I arrived at the office my student told me that it was minus 23 Celsius outside. I asked her to put the kettle on. Mercifully, she did.

But, like I say, the summers: roasting! This was a natural invitation for me to get out and about to see more of this incredible country. Sometimes, at the weekends, I just got on buses and went wherever they were going. It didn't matter, it was all new. I kept a full-sized national map folded up in my rucksack and winged it. That's a good way to travel!

Now, whilst at Manchester University, I had studied a module on the Holocaust and the Final Solution in Eastern Europe. Unsurprisingly, there were monuments, both large and small,

all around Poland, commemorating related incidents which had taken place during World War Two. It was interesting to see them, and also to have some of the locals translate the inscriptions for me. It was mind-boggling in many ways. The human species has such an astonishing capacity for the destruction of its own kind. It beggars belief.

But as a historian, I was naturally interested. There was a signpost a few hundred yards from my flat in Ostrów indicating that the site of the Nazi extermination camp, Treblinka, was only about twenty kilometres away. I'd always had a certain trepidation about visiting places of that kind, but also a curiosity just to see them.

So, one Saturday morning I put on shorts and a T-shirt, covered myself in sunblock, and set out on my bike. That part of the country was very flat, and cycling was a breeze. I cycled through the forest just outside the town and crossed a railway line at Małkinia Górna. I then turned right onto one of the roughest coccyx-shattering roads I have ever encountered! It had been a while since I'd been on a bike, and I'd forgotten that this could happen. This must have been how Jim Dale felt after he'd done the trolley-down-the-staircase stunt in *Carry On Again Doctor* whilst playing Dr Nookey.

But, right then, a flash of revelation hit me. I grabbed hold of my brake levers and screeched to a gravel-splitting halt. It occurred to me that there was no way I could enter a memorial site such as Treblinka. Not like this. I glanced down at my T-shirt of the day. Slayer. The European Campaign shirt. The bootleg one I'd picked up after the *Clash of the Titans* gig in Birmingham. Oops! I'd put it on without thinking. It was clean and had been the first one out of the drawer that morning. But the imagery on this shirt, coupled with this location, simply did not match up in my mind. Slayer's lyrics, dating back to when they released their *Reign in Blood* album in 1986, had often addressed German involvement in World War Two. Their track 'Angel of Death' was about Dr Mengele; and

'Behind the Crooked Cross' was said to concern the Wehrmacht as it launched its attacks through Eastern Europe. Slayer's lyrical imagery sometimes translated itself onto their tour shirts. There were aspects of this imagery on the one I was wearing as I stood alongside my bike looking at the potholed single-track road ahead of me. Some may have said, 'Hey, Phil. It's just a T-shirt. Come on. What difference does it make?' But I couldn't quite square that circle myself. Entering a location such as Treblinka in this garb? No, just no. It would have been the equivalent of visiting the Sistine Chapel wearing a Cradle of Filth T-shirt and an inverted cross pendant. I turned my handlebars around and pensively headed back towards my flat.

*

A few weeks later, the subject of the camps came up at the end of an elementary-level language class. I explained that I was interested in seeing Treblinka but hadn't yet brought myself to go. After the class, one of the older students, who was actually a science teacher in an adjoining town, stayed back. She explained that she could arrange to take me there and show me the monuments.

The following Saturday afternoon, she and her husband, who spoke only Polish and German, and I, who spoke only English, took the fifteen-minute drive up to the site. We spent an hour or so looking around at the inscribed granite memorial stones. She then explained to me, in broken English but clearly enough, that her grandfather on her mother's side was one of the people who had been rounded up in 1943. I looked at her, shocked out of my wits. She just shrugged her shoulders and cocked her head, as if to say, 'Well, what can you do?' She then took a couple of steps away from me and said a brief prayer.

Situations like that really do put things into perspective.

We headed back to Ostrów in silence.

Buckcherry	'Slit My Wrists'
Children of Bodom	'Everytime I Die'
Doro	'Long Way Home'
	'Love Me in Black'
Dream Theater	'Hollow Years'
	'Peruvian Skies'
Mötley Crüe	'Afraid'
	'Bitter Pill'
Nickelback	'How You Remind Me'
Nightwish	'Bless the Child'
	'Ever Dream'
Vader	'Epitaph'
W.A.S.P.	'Hallowed Ground'
	'My Wicked Heart'
Yngwie Malmsteen	'End of My Rope'

CHAPTER 19

'From England, aye?'

If any of you out there have ever considered a career in drinking, a good place to get into training would be Glasgow. I feel that I can confidently say, without any fear of contradiction, that Glasgow is the drinkingest city I have ever lived in.

I first visited Glasgow in 2004 and, having disembarked at the train station, I was feeling a bit arid. Walking along the platform edge towards the main exit, I glanced at a signboard which was placed high up in one of the gantries. A large and very conspicuous sign stated: *'The Solid Rock Café. It almost makes you feel sorry for other pubs!'* I stopped for a second. Solid Rock? Wasn't that an old Dire Straits track? Interesting introduction for a newcomer to the city. But seeing as I had a bit of time on my hands, I thought I would seek it out and mosey on in there.

I headed down the escalators and spotted the Solid literally a stone's throw from the station. I then ran the gauntlet of Hope Street, stealthily dodging a stampede of taxis and buses. There was an A-frame blackboard standing outside the Solid's door, and the surface of the board was covered with tiny writing. It could have been written using the end of a Tipp-Ex brush. I bent down to take a closer look. What was the story here? And then the light dawned. In minuscule lettering, listed from A to Z, and completely covering the board from top to bottom, were the names of just about every metal and rock band I had ever heard of, and a lot more besides! I just stood there staring at it for a while. Was this genuine? Could this be for real? Had I seriously happened upon a pub which basically played this kind of music, as a point of principle, all day long?

This all sounded far too good to be true. But just in case, I thought I'd best take a wee look…

I pushed the door open and entered a dark cavernous bar which reached way back into the building. But the first thing that struck me was not the low lighting, the picture discs plastered up on the walls, or the congregation of long-haired metal fans sitting at the bar or generally hanging around drinking beers and chatting: the first thing that hit me was the track 'Hell Ain't a Bad Place to Be' by AC/DC, which was being played through the house speakers. I stood still for a moment with my eyes wide whilst I tried to take this place in. This didn't look contrived. It didn't seem as though this was a one-off track, and that I had just happened to arrive whilst it was playing. The Solid Rock Café appeared to be completely authentic: a proper heavy metal pub! And this was underlined when I turned to my left and saw the big screen TV which was silently showing an old Iron Maiden video.

I had hit upon some kind of metal heartland here. And there was no need for me to pinch myself; I knew I was awake.

I walked up to the bar and surveyed the drinks on offer. There were the inevitable pints of course, but also a mountainous quantity of spirits, shooters, whiskeys, vodkas, rums, etc. I decided to play it safe and go for a pint.

A very tall, black-clad barman with extremely spiky hair appeared in front of me. He was sporting a welcoming *How can I help you?* expression. I placed my order.

'Afternoon, mate. A pint of bitter please.' He gave me a big cheesy smile and began pulling the beer.

Two big, heavy-set blokes who were sitting at the bar just to my left started sniggering and looking at the guy behind the bar with knowing expressions. I stared straight ahead. I thought it was probably for the best. New kid in town and all that.

'A pint of *bitter*. The man here wants a pint of *bitter*. Pour him a pint of *bitter* will ya, Kenny?' There was more giggling and spluttering.

The bloke who was nearer to me put his hand on my shoulder, leaned in towards me and said, 'From England, aye?'

'Aye, that's right.'

'Okay.' More snorts. 'Y-Y-You don't call it bitter here, pal. Up here, it's heavy.'

'It's what?'

'Heavy. You ask for a pint of heavy.'

'Heavy bitter?'

At this point his mate completely lost it, slammed his hands down on the bar and burst out into completely uncontrolled hysterics.

'No, no. No, man, just heavy. Okay?'

'Okay then.' I glanced back at Kenny and said, 'A heavy...?'

Kenny, having poured my first ever heavy, plopped it down on the bar and gave me a look as if to say, *Don't worry about it, these two are full of shite.*

'You wanting another couple of sambucas, guys?' Kenny piped up.

The two blokes looked up in unison, focusing on the question. 'Aww, I don't know, pal,' said one of them. 'We're getting a wee bit blootered here. But, go on.'

Two more were poured, and the guys looked at them, clearly wondering now if this had been a wise decision. They shot them down and both reacted with teeth-bared, nostril-flaring expressions which appeared to border on pain.

They then decided that their time was up, and that they actually had other things to be doing with their afternoon. The one that had been talking to me reached over, put his hand on my shoulder again, and slurred: 'Hey, no offence, mate. We're all pals in here. But the way you asked for that pint? I almost pished in my jeans!'

He then said to his companion, who was now starting to look a bit peaky, 'Come on, we've got to get out of here for once. Shift yerself.'

His mate didn't even turn around to look at him. His eyes were completely glazed, and they appeared to be fixed on some obscure point in the distance. 'Naw, I think I may hang around just a wee bit longer.'

'How? We've got to get on up the road. Come on.'

'I would, mate... but, shite... ah cannae move!'

At that point, Kenny decided to intervene and helped with propping up duties. The two guys shuffled out, still giggling and snorting.

Kenny dusted off his hands and turned to me.

'Aye, he's right. It's heavy. But call it whatever you like. Just be yourself. All's fair in the Solid!'

In spite of this slightly weird introduction to the Solid Rock Café, I was starting to feel quite at home. I had been in Glasgow for all of about ten minutes, and most of that had been spent in a pub, but I already had a feeling that things were going to work out.

I then decided to go out on a limb and make a very important enquiry: 'Good. Cool. Excellent. I'm Phil, by the way. Now, I've just got to get something clear: is this an *actual* heavy metal pub? I saw the sign in the train station, and the board outside. Do you really, seriously, play all that stuff in here every day?'

'Aye. That we do. Anything you'd like to hear?'

Kenny showed me a screen which was placed up behind the far end of the bar. There was a playlist on it, packed tight from top to bottom. So, just by way of a random suggestion, I said: 'Anything by Motörhe...?' But before I could even finish, the massive opening chord of 'Killed by Death' knifed its way out of the speakers. No sooner said than done!

I ordered another heavy.

*

The real reason behind my appearance in Glasgow was not to spend the rest of my life examining the world through the bottom of a pint glass: I had gone there to do a postgraduate course in War Studies at the university. It sounded like a fascinating course, and I immersed myself from day one.

I found somewhere to live and spent a couple of years sharing a flat with Vikki, who was pretty connected in Glasgow's goth scene, and Mark, who was originally from Norwich and was a massive Foo Fighters fan. This sounded like a good set-up, and it was, especially when I look back at my time in Huddersfield. We all became regulars at the Solid.

And Glasgow's metal scene was raging! In fact, I would say that Glasgow is also the metalest city I have ever lived in. If bands were on tour, they would play Glasgow rather than Edinburgh. Glasgow had the venues, huge hordes of metal fans of all persuasions, and, of course, the Solid, which advertised all the upcoming metal shows. There were also a couple of local bands that were starting out at the time: Attica Rage, who played old-school heavy metal and included their version of Iron Maiden's 'Fear of the Dark' in their set; and Achren, who were, at the time, a three-piece black metal band: two guitars, drums, vocals – no bass.

Sometimes I would just take a chance on a band that looked interesting without necessarily knowing anything about it. The first metal gig I went to in Glasgow was advertised through a poster on the wall of the Solid. Månegarm. I wasn't familiar with

Månegarm. But their logo was sufficiently spiky to imply death metal, or potentially black metal. That was as much information as I required. They were playing at the Òran Mór, which, outwardly, appeared to be a church but was now a bar. The venue itself was downstairs in what presumably had been the crypt. A very suitable location for a night of extreme metal. Achren blazed out the support set.

There was also the Barrowlands, which was a really popular venue for fans on account of its springy floor. When a mosh pit got going, such as when I saw Megadeth there on their *United Abominations* tour in 2007, the floor became a huge strutted trampoline. Most Glaswegians that I've spoken to about gigs have consistently said that the Barrowlands was the best venue in which to see any band.

Additionally, there was The Garage on Sauchiehall Street in the city centre. Metal bands used this venue as a regular stop, and it was there that I saw Tesla for the first time with a pal of mine, and fellow regular at the Solid, called Don. Don was a huge Frank Hannon fan, and he made sure that we got right up to the barrier for that one.

The Garage was also W.A.S.P.'s regular stop. I got to see them there several times on different tours, but the best occasion was when they reprised their 1992 *Crimson Idol* album complete with its accompanying film. Don, who was also a massive W.A.S.P. fan, practically went spare when he heard that this was happening. On the night, we drank a tankful down at the Solid, and then went nuts in the crowd to tracks like 'Chainsaw Charlie', 'I Am One', 'The Arena of Pleasure', and 'The Great Misconceptions of Me'. We absolutely got what those tracks were saying, and we had one of the best nights of old-school metal of our lives!

In Glasgow there were gig venues everywhere. There was something going on every single night, and if you wanted to see live music, just about every taste under the sun was catered for.

But I did have a personal favourite venue, and it suited what I was into perfectly. This one was called the Soundhaus. This was a particular spot for fans of extreme underground metal. Bands such as Behemoth from Poland and Destruction from Germany would play the Soundhaus. The venue itself was part of an old factory building, much of which looked as though it was semi-derelict. The gig room was downstairs in a really tight space with a low ceiling. There were no windows and barely even any air vents. Sufferers of claustrophobia would certainly not have felt at home in there. But I thought it was great! The place had a dark subterranean feel to it, absolutely befitting the bands who performed there.

It was in the Soundhaus that I saw Vader, the Polish death metal band I started listening to whilst I was living in their own country a few years earlier. The gig was, naturally, advertised in the Solid. I signed up for that one right away.

On the night of the gig, I headed down to the venue after finishing a day at work. I got changed into appropriate gear in the office toilets before actually going. Showing up in a suit would not have been appropriate. So off I went to join the black T-shirt brigade queuing up outside the venue.

After shuffling through the narrow dark tunnel which led to the gig room, I picked a suitable T-shirt from the merch dude and headed off to the bar to get a bottle of water. It used to get so stuffy in the Soundhaus that water was my usual drink of choice. The support band was Belphegor, from Austria. They had been around since the early 1990s, but I'd never actually heard of them. You know how it is? You can't listen to everything! Having got up on the stage, they certainly looked the part: long-haired, clad in black, and brandishing black guitars with inverted headstocks. The thing that struck me about them firstly though was their drummer. He was tiny! He couldn't have been more than about five feet tall, and he could have hidden behind a blade of grass! But as Belphegor ripped into their set, this guy showed what he was made of. He pummelled his way through the music like a demon and kept the blast beating rhythms metronomically perfect. What a player!

And then it was Vader's turn, and chants of 'Piotr, Piotr, Piotr' started to rise from the crowd. It was clear that quite a lot of Poles, who weren't professedly metal fans, had turned up anyway. The majority of them were young girls who looked like they had dressed for a night in a more salubrious venue, but they were there nonetheless. Good stuff. Well done them!

Vader all but destroyed the Soundhaus with their set. They started with 'Epitaph' from the *Revelations* album, which created a huge circle pit in front of the stage; but when they played 'Helleluyah!!! (God is Dead)', it felt like the place was set to descend straight down to the pits of Dante's Inferno. The audience, myself included, went psychotic. This was blatant, unbridled mercilessness, and it was unbelievable! And what did this Polish quartet finish off their set with? What else but cover versions of 'Black Sabbath' and 'Raining Blood'! By the end, I was bruised, battered and generally knocked about. Someone, I think accidentally, had put a right cross into my jaw at some point. That's the mosh pit for you.

But I did need a certain amount of recuperation time. I called in sick to work the following day, citing bad guts. The truth, however, was that I was utterly, utterly fucked!

*

One day, Vikki mentioned that Glasgow also had a club called the Cathouse. Cathouse? That rang a bell. Wasn't the Cathouse the name of one of the clubs that featured in Penelope Spheeris's film *The Decline of Western Civilisation, Part II*? I hit my memory's rewind switch, and yep, there it was. The Cathouse section of the film had featured footage of Faster Pussycat cranking out 'Bathroom Wall' and also a track actually called 'Cathouse', to a packed hall. By this point, I had partially made my peace with glam metal. (It wasn't so bad after all. Well, some of it wasn't.) Faster Pussycat looked amazing on stage in that movie, and Poison's banter stole the show.

But, anyway, back to the Cathouse in Glasgow.

Vikki had told me that it was a rock club, so it had naturally registered, but I just hadn't got round to going there yet. But then one evening, after a research session down at the university library, I just happened to be heading home via Union Street. I stopped outside the club's main door and checked my watch. It was about nine o'clock, and I didn't really have anything else to do at the time. So, nothing ventured nothing gained, I headed in. And when I got in, I was greeted with a joyous sound. The DJ was blasting out 'War Ensemble' by Slayer! I hadn't expected *that!* I was anticipating Pantera, or Nirvana or Soundgarden. But genuine old-school thrash metal? That didn't get played in clubs anymore, did it? Well, clearly, in Glasgow it did. I was having flashbacks to the Rockhouse in Derby. But the Cathouse was almost empty. It was a Wednesday night, and a sleepy one at that. That was fine with me. I had the entire mosh pit to myself, and I made use of every square inch of it. And that was before I'd even got to the bar!

Attica Rage	'Road Dog'
Belphegor	'The Ancient Enemy'
Buckcherry	'Crazy Bitch'
George Thorogood	'Get a Haircut'
Iron Maiden	'The Clansman'
Judas Priest	'Judas Rising'
Megadeth	'Washington Is Next!'
Mötley Crüe	'You're All I Need'
	'She Goes Down'
Motörhead	'Get Back in Line'
	'Just 'Cos You Got the Power'
Rage	'Long Hard Road'
Tesla	'Cumin' Atcha Live'
Wildhearts	'The Miles Away Girl'
Vader	'Helleluyah!!! (God is Dead)'

CHAPTER 20

I had gone completely Gary Moore

Meanwhile, Vikki had started seeing a guy called Iain whom she'd met on a night out. Iain was a really nice bloke, a real gent, and a very handy chef. He was able to cobble together amazing meals, sometimes out of the most meagre ingredients. Additionally, he was the singer in a local metal band called Blood Drum. They weren't signed, but they were playing a few gigs around Glasgow and had a bit of a following. So I started following them as well. Hugh, or Shug as he was known to his mates, was the guitarist, and he was quite a handy player. He clearly knew what he was doing with riffs and solos. They seemed to pour out of him.

Blood Drum had written a track called 'Wildwood Blues', which was based on Jack London's book *The Call of the Wild*, and this was the centrepiece of their set. It started off with Iain sending out a crazed howl through the PA, and then the band kicked into a track which was bordering on prog rock, there were so many parts to it. When they played this one live, Iain would get off the stage and stalk his way around the audience with his microphone, bellowing out the vocals to individuals. Not many frontmen did that, and it looked great. You never quite knew who's face he was going to get into.

I saw them gig a few times in venues such as Ivory Blacks and The Vale, but Blood Drum was starting to fold. They had had a second guitarist, but he was rarely around, and maybe things were just grinding to a halt. That often occurs with unsigned bands, even good ones; they just stop happening and cease to be.

But Iain was interested in keeping things going. He asked me if I'd like to be part of a new band which would carry on playing some of Blood Drum's music but also start putting together its own. As I'm sure you can appreciate by now, this didn't require much thought on my part. So, I was in. But there were only two of us. Not the ideal number of members for a metal band, but at least it was the germ of something.

We started casting around online for other members, and we found another guitarist who lived in Paisley. Excellent! Things were beginning to come together nicely. This guy had even recorded a complete album on Pro Tools, and by the sound of his playing he would fit in well. He was a riffer and a shredder, and also a good vocalist. That could be handy for harmonies. Maybe. We also found a drummer, Paul, who had played in a few bands around Glasgow, most recently Dirty Cannon, which was named after a Glaswegian porn cinema that had been closed down a few years earlier.

We all exchanged phone numbers and email addresses and arranged to jam the following week.

The first rehearsal room we found was built into a railway tunnel near Glasgow Central train station. It was cheap, very cheap, and maybe that should have been a giveaway. It was entered through an unmarked white door on the inside of the tunnel arch, which looked suspect in itself. You had to bang on it with your fist in order to get anyone to open it up! Also, the nearest car park was about a quarter of a mile away, and Glaswegian parking fees were up there with those of capital cities.

The rehearsal room itself was massive. It was a huge whitewashed cavern with amps, cables, and a drum kit. This was all good so far. The problem, however, was that it was clearly a breeding ground for flies. They were bloody everywhere! The critters were skittering around on the walls, buzzing in our faces, and generally making a pain in the arse of themselves. There were a number of black splats on the walls; evidence that they had been a pain in the arse for others too.

Paul was awesome! He was like a long-lost mate who had reappeared after years of being away. There were big handshakes and cheesy grins. And, I seem to recall, he was sporting an Iron Maiden shirt. What's more, shit, he could play the drums! He hit like a depth charge! All I needed to do was crank out a riff from off the top of my head, and he would be right on it. He was able to turn anything into metal, and he loved getting his head down and blasting out four-four beats, with fills and cymbal crashes loaded in.

Paul wasn't a subtle player. He was a kit destroyer and a stick splitter. The shards of wood that piled up under the kit after he had been on it could have been bagged up and sold as kindling. I can't count the number of times we were blasting through 'No Voices in the Sky' or 'The Wicker Man', and we'd have to stop: 'Ah *shite*, there goes another stick!' He always brought an array of spares.

The guitar player from Paisley though? He didn't show up. Iain called him to find out what was what. Apparently, he couldn't get to the rehearsal because of something to do with work and/or his girlfriend. Fair enough, these things can happen. Perhaps next week then. Or rather, perhaps not. He had completely gone to ground. We neither heard from him nor saw him ever again. Okay, bum deal. No point in chasing shadows. It would be a one guitar band then. So be it.

That evening, with just Iain, Paul and me in the rehearsal room, we ended up writing most of a track which we would later play in our set. It just cropped up. I was basically jamming out a bunch of power chords in a fairly Neanderthal manner, when Paul cottoned right on and started blasting. 'Hey, Phil, that's a rockin' tune, mate! What is it?'

'This? No idea really. Just a few chords. Something to jam to, you know.' Paul definitely had a point though. 'But yeah, you're right. Maybe we should remember this one and work on it a bit.'

Iain was up for it as well. I'd seen his foot tapping and his head nodding. A grin was spreading across his face. There was a serious groove going down under the railway bridge that night!

We must have jammed for a couple of hours, and we played as though we were in front of a packed arena. We slammed through a few cover versions and stuff we made up on the spot. By the time we had finished, we were dripping and knackered. We called it an evening and decided that we were certainly going to make this a regular thing. We packed up our gear and cleared up the shards of devastated drumsticks. Having paid the guy who was running the place (or at least hanging around in there – we never found out all that much about him), we headed back to our respective pads.

Back at my flat in the south of Glasgow, I was buzzing! That was probably the best jam session I had ever played in. My fingertips were wrecked from all the power chords, string bending and tapping, but who cared? I was, as they say, stoked to the max!

I just needed a solo to put into the track that we'd been working on. It was an all-out metal track, so a ripping solo would be obligatory. We didn't have any verses or choruses yet, so I didn't know where it would fit in, but I decided to work on something anyway.

Things were going along nicely, but we were still minus a bass player.

Iain had something up his sleeve on that score. He had a pal called John, and he called him up. And the following week, he was there. John was great and was a perfect fit for what we needed. He'd played in a few bands before, so he knew how things worked and had one or two contacts. Interestingly, he was also heavily into World War Two battle re-enactments. He played the role of a Wehrmacht soldier, so actually spent quite a lot of the time getting shot!

We jammed week after week, playing old Blood Drum stuff and making up our own.

Gradually things started to come together, and it was gig time. But, as yet, the band didn't have a name. That can be a problem when you want to sign up to play at a venue. You can't just present yourselves anonymously. That's not how it works. Picture the scene with a promoter:

Promoter: 'So, you're a new local metal band. Great, excellent. Let's get you on the bill as the openers next Saturday night. Right, guys, what are you called?'

Numpty: 'Eh?'

Promoter: 'Your band. What's it called?'

Numpty: 'Err, well, I dunno. Y'see, we don't have a name. Or at least not yet. Is that important...?'

Promoter: 'Err, well, yes. Pretty basic when you think about it.'

Numpty: 'Ooh, we haven't really got to that stage yet.'

Promoter: 'Well all right, but what are we going to call you? We'll need to know who you are so we can put your name on the tickets.'

Numpty: 'Ah, yes, good point. We'll need to think about that one.'

Promoter: 'That's right. You will. And fast. You'll need to be called *something* in order to get on the bill. I don't really care what you're called, and you can change your name later anyway. You'd better get your skulls together on this one... Otherwise, see ya!'

We juggled a few ideas around for a while and then just decided to use the name of an old Blood Drum song: 'Sky9'. Not bad. A band name with a number in it. That would stand out.

We got ourselves a booking at Nice N Sleazy, a city centre basement venue. I'd seen a few bands in there before. A few years earlier, I'd seen Dan Baird from the Georgia Satellites with his current band, Homemade Sin, in Sleazy. So this was the real thing: a proper venue with a sound desk, lights, monitors, the lot. In the past I'd done some open mike stuff in pubs and taken a shot at tracks like 'Runaway Train' by Soul Asylum and 'King's Highway' by Tom Petty, but this was something else.

The only condition was that we needed to sell a given number of tickets for the promoter to deem us worthy: about twenty, I think. Hardly big numbers that were likely to be clamouring for an encore after we'd opened the night with half an hour of unknown tracks and a cover version. But still, a smattering of punters. So we started touting them around work and to other people we knew who may have been interested in an evening of live metal. Between us we managed to drum up about thirty.

We all arrived early on the night with our gear checked, fresh strings, lots of extra drumsticks, and spare guitars just in case. After faffing around for a while, we got up on stage and did a soundcheck. Everything was working fine, so we were all done in about ten minutes. So, back to faffing, this time upstairs at the bar. One thing I learned very quickly was that, even if you were in a band that was playing that night, you would spend ninety per cent of your time at a venue hanging around, and only about ten per cent actually on the stage.

After what felt like hours, it was time to head back down into the basement. We were all really fired up for the night. This was our debut, and we were going to let folk know we had arrived. The stage was all ready for us. The drums were set up, guitars were poised on their stands, and the sound guy was behind his desk. We stepped up onto the stage and took a look around. There were quite a few people there, more than we'd expected. Not a bad turnout, in fact. A friend of Iain's, a photographer called Emmett, had also come, and he'd brought some of his gear with him. He was planning on taking a few snaps.

I strapped my black B.C. Rich Stealth over my shoulder, and John slung on his bass. Paul got comfortable behind the kit and smacked out a few test blasts on the snare, and Iain grabbed hold of the mike with both hands.

And then the stage lights came on, and the audience completely disappeared. That's something that audience members don't realise: quite often, bands can't see them. The stage lights in Nice N Sleazy were so bright that we could barely see beyond the lip of the stage. Maybe I should have worn shades. We looked across at each other. Ready? Right. This is for real. Paul clicked out four on his sticks.

Blam! We were off! We all went for it, full throttle and full bore!

God knows what my mates from work were thinking. They knew me as the sort of bloke who was usually quite mellow and chilled out. They may well have thought that I'd taken a shot of Dr Jekyll's potion and turned into a kind of frenzied maniac! First-timer support bands are usually known for being self-effacing and a bit coy on stage. Not Sky9 though. We stepped on the gas and redlined everything. We all worked on a principle which I'd had in my head for years: *play it like you mean it!*

I had a row of pedals at my feet. There was a delay, a flanger, a wah-wah, and the most powerful distortion pedal I could find in the shops. I gave them all a good stomping. What I should have done though was prioritise my tuner pedal. Part way through our second track, it dawned on me that my low E string had slipped down to something like D flat. Oops. New strings you see? I hadn't played them in properly. Rookie mistake.

We shredded through our set and, although some of our songs weren't even fully written at that stage, they all took off and landed quite nicely. Iain did his prowling around the audience thing, and

I was throwing every shape possible. Paul's drums were right on it, and John laid down bass lines as thick as concrete. We tore through five tracks and finished off with a version of 'Paranoid' which featured a solo played with my foot flat on the wah-wah pedal. What we didn't know was that Emmett had been darting around in front of the stage for most of the gig taking photographs. We couldn't see him.

I came off stage dripping with sweat and feeling more electrified than I ever had before in my life. I literally felt like I was high, and that I could have taken on the entire planet! But, before that, I needed a drink. Alongside being drenched, I was also parched. Gigging is thirsty work, especially when you put so much ferocity into it.

And we went down well.

There were three other bands on the bill after us, and the guitar player from one of them came up to me. 'Bloody hell, pal. That was fucking *awesome!* Where the hell did you learn to play like that?'

'I don't really know, mate. It just sort of comes to me, and when it works, it *works*. That felt bloody brilliant. I can't believe how amazing that was. Hey, check it out, I'm practically bleeding shaking!'

The guy took a glance back at the stage, and said, 'Look, I don't want to get on your case or anything, and feel free to say "no", but could I use your amp for our set? The sound you got out of that Blackstar was fantastic!'

'Sure you can. No problem. Plug into it and let it rip. Just one thing though, please don't knock any beer over it.'

'Ah, thanks so much, mate, and don't worry about it, I'll leave my pint right here. How long have you guys been together, by the way?'

'Only about two or three months probably. Something like that. This was our first proper gig.'

'Fucking hell! You're shitting me! Your *first* gig? No way!'

'Way!'

He nodded. 'You guys have set the bar pretty high tonight. Nice one!'

*

Gigging was the best buzz I had ever had in my life! The rush of the sound, the power of the blast which shot out from the band and filled the room, and the amazing sense of power that accompanied it was incredible. I felt shot through with an electricity which woke up every single part of me. Absolutely mind-blowing!

It was only afterwards, when Emmett had forwarded the photos he had taken, that I realised I was one of those guitar players who couldn't control his facial expressions whilst playing. In most of the pictures it looked as though I was either enjoying a pleasurable moment, sniffing a bucket of fish heads, or chewing a hornet. Unbeknownst to me, I had gone completely Gary Moore!

But the experience gave me more than just that primal buzz. Gigging gave me a more critical eye when watching bands, especially young and unsigned bands, on stage. I learned to appreciate how good a lot of them really are and how much work goes into putting on a show, irrespective of the small numbers that turn up to see them. And it's not just the playing on the night: it's the rehearsing, the writing of the music and lyrics, and the ability to play together at a level which is often underestimated and underappreciated. It's also the tenacity to get out there and gig. None of these guys are going to have roadies. Everyone has to do the heavy lifting of amps, drum kits, and other gear – set it all up, and then take it all down again. This is all for just a few quid per gig, or maybe a free beer tab. It takes a hell of a lot of commitment, and you have to really mean it.

And occasionally you encounter that tosser in the crowd – you know, the bloke (and it usually is a bloke) who can't keep his mouth shut. It's easy to point the finger and go, 'Ah, yeah, you! You're shite! Get off!' Most folk who do this have never been on stage and faced the venue from the opposite direction. Pointing your finger at a band is one thing; it takes an altogether different kind of balls to be in that band and ignore or face these guys down.

Of course, there are other methods. The Nikki Sixx approach would be to dive off the stage and clatter the offending dickhead in the teeth with the business end of a bass! We all have our different styles…

Anthrax	'Antisocial'
Black Label Society	'Fire It Up'
Bolt Thrower	'The Killchain'
Iron Maiden	'The Wicker Man'
	'These Colours Don't Run'
Kreator	'From Flood into Fire'
	'Voices of the Dead'
Motörhead	'Keys to the Kingdom'
	'No Voices in the Sky'
Nightwish	'Alpenglow'
	'Élan'
Therapy?	'Screamager'
The Almighty	'Little Lost Sometimes'
W.A.S.P.	'Heaven's Hung in Black'
Within Temptation	'Shot in the Dark'

CHAPTER 21

Santie

'Holy moly! That guy must get through guitar strings faster than I get through underwear!'

That's not the kind of thing you hear every day now, is it?

But, there again, Santie isn't the kind of woman you run into every day either.

We were in the car and heading into Edinburgh on the way to the cinema. We were going to see part one of the new version of *IT* by Stephen King. Slayer was on the car stereo, and Kerry King had just torn into his guitar solo in 'Angel of Death'. It was fortunate that we were waiting at a red light, because if we'd been in full flow, I would probably have stacked the car up in a ditch whilst howling in gobsmacked hysterics.

A few minutes later, however, we arrived at the flicks fully intact, undented, and with our insurance policy unblemished.

I had met Santie the year before, and we hit it off immediately. This was the real thing, there was no doubt about that. She was tall and elegant, and always wore a sunny smile; and with her wiggling walk and giggling talk, I honestly didn't stand a chance. I was hooked!

And, what's more, Santie had one or two extra tricks up her sleeve. Chief amongst these was that she rode horses; and not only that, she rode dressage horses. That takes some doing, believe me! She had been working as a riding teacher and as a tack shop manager in South Africa for a couple of decades before I even knew she existed. At one point, she was even approached by a branch of the Gauteng police and asked if she would train the horses and riders in one of their mounted divisions. So, to put it mildly, she could not only talk the talk, she could trot, canter and gallop it as well.

The first time I went to visit her at her flat in Edinburgh, she showed me her impressive Stephen King collection; and then, whilst we blethered on about the *Dark Tower* books, we realised that dinner had become a bit charred.

Plan B?

The pub of course!

We headed downstairs and she showed me to her car. We got comfy and she turned the ignition key. As she did so, Def Leppard's 'Photograph' shot out of the speakers! She gave me a big grin, as if to say, *I'm into this stuff as well.* Then she rammed up the volume and booted the accelerator. That's my girl!

*

If you've ever been anywhere near horses, you'll know that there is far more to them than meets the eye. They are certainly not one-size-fits-all characters. For one thing, there is the mare (often contrary, opinionated, and prone to a nip and the odd buck here and there); and there's the gelding (a bit more chilled, usually fairly amenable and pragmatic). And, of course, there's the Shetland Pony – oh, so cute – but likely to be right royal shits at the same time, and extremely adept at busting out of paddocks.

One of the problems is that all, or sometimes none, of these factors can come into play. You just never know, and you have to keep your wits about you in stable yards, because, believe me, those horses are watching your every move and are constantly on the lookout for any treats you may have hidden in your pockets.

Glamourous it ain't. Coming home in the evening following a full day of doing all things horsey caked in crap, hay, mud and horse snot is not an uncommon occurrence. In fact, if you're doing it properly, it's all part of the gig!

And we mustn't forget that all horses, irrespective of size, sex or breed, regularly produce prodigious quantities of shite.

Inevitably, having spent a full day dealing with such matters (and having shaken all the hay out of her boots), Santie's first port of call upon getting home was always the bath. She usually got back from work at about half past eight in the evening, and I would make sure the bath was prepared and ready to go. That bath would be hot, loaded with bubbles, and the bathroom would be lit with candles.

And so it was on this occasion.

During her regular luxuriating sessions in the tub, I would usually be getting on with something else. It would be the evening, and therefore chill time. More often than not, I'd plug in my guitar and blast out a few riffs and solos; or I might do a spot of tidying up; or maybe I'd just sit down and read a book. This time though, I was listening to music in the kitchen and sorting out the evening's repast.

I was about halfway through doing this and taking a break in the living room when Santie stepped out of the bathroom in her dressing gown. She had a surprised and slightly concerned expression on her face. She called out and waved her hands, beckoning me over to where she was standing. I walked over to her wondering what could be up. She then stepped right up to me and whispered in my ear: 'There's an angry man in the kitchen – he's screaming his head off about something!'

She stepped back and looked at me, her hands clasped together. Her brow was slightly furrowed in apprehension.

At first, I wasn't quite sure what she had said. 'There's a what?'

'He's in the kitchen. He sounds horribly upset. I can't tell what he's going on about, but he sounds terribly wound up about something or other.'

I took a step back and thought about what I had just heard. Was this a cause for concern?

'An angry man. An *angry* man? In the kitchen? Why would there be an angry man in the kitchen? The only man that's been in there recently is me, and I'm, well, you know, quite mellow, and... oh, hang on, I think I catch your drift now.'

Whilst Santie had been in the tub, I'd been slicing and dicing things for dinner. I'd also been reminiscing on Bathory. I had put their entire *The Return* album on YouTube and had decided that it needed to be turned right up. There's zero point in playing an album like that quietly. It's authentic Scandinavian black metal, and it demands full volume.

What I hadn't taken into account was that this kind of music is something of an acquired taste, and it isn't for everybody. All told, it's pretty hefty stuff!

We walked into the kitchen together.

'Wow, he's certainly going for it, isn't he?' Santie pointed out.

'Oh yes, I guess you could say that. I'll turn it down a wee bit, shall I? How about that?' Quorthon was, at that point, heaving out 'The Wind of Mayhem', and things were starting to get a bit turbulent. He did, indeed, sound quite angry.

'Thank you, that's better. But, no, no, don't turn it off! If this is your thing, that's fine. It's just a bit, well, erm, *too* heavy. Don't get me wrong, but all I'm hearing is *UUUURRRRGGHH! AAARRRRGGGHHH! OORRRRGGGHHHH!* That doesn't really do it for me.'

'I see.'

'If you want to put on Queen or Bon Jovi or Meat Loaf, go for it. Crank the hell out of it! But, wow, this. What *is* this?' She checked the screen on the computer. 'Bathory. Hmm, yeah. It's just a little bit, well... scary...'

But Santie only needed to point out one other issue: 'Just one thing though, please don't play this with the windows open. If any horses hear it, they'll crap themselves and go bonkers!'

Fair play to her though. She didn't boot the daylights out of the speakers in the way that kid from school had when he first encountered Quorthon's rasping tones!

*

With Santie, the world opened up. We travelled. Since I'd come back from Poland, I'd barely even touched my passport. I was quite happy in Scotland. It had all the mountains, lochs, coastlines, islands, castles, and wildlife I could ever desire – right on my doorstep. I took Santie away on regular trips around the country and showed her as much as I could. This was all fine, but Santie broadened my horizons. Within a year of meeting her, my passport had been thoroughly examined, or at least casually glanced at, in several international airports, as we went on tours of the Netherlands, Venice, and South Africa. She reminded me of the simple truth that there really is a wonderful world out there; you've just got to reach out and touch it.

It was following a holiday in 2017 that I decided I had to pop the question. We'd been on a cruising tour around Iceland, and I'd been limbering up to the moment evening after evening whilst on board. Somehow, the opportunity kept eluding me.

But having got back on terra firma, that was it. Tonight was the night! This absolutely had to happen!

Back up in her flat in Edinburgh, I told Santie that I had a surprise for her. Her interest was piqued. I'd actually bought her a horse. Not a real one you understand. That would have been a nightmare to box up and wrap! But a nicely sculpted model of a trotting Thoroughbred. It was her birthday after all. And then, having rehearsed the moment thousands of times, as simply as I could, I asked her to marry me...

Santie took a step back and looked at me with an expression of completely undiluted shock, as though I had just suggested the idea of doing something utterly degrading. She then gave me a huge smile, rested her head on my shoulder and whispered, 'Yes, of course I will.'

*

Then things started to race: 'save the date' cards shot out in all directions; we did cake tastings; we visited florists, and Santie decided that she fancied tulips; and then, naturally, the dress. We also started making wine charms and all sorts of other things which involved scissors, tweezers and lots of red ribbon.

And, as you would expect, at a wedding such as ours, the music was going to be fundamental.

We didn't fancy the idea of hiring a DJ. They usually just play what they want to play, all night, rather than what you actually want for a party. So we scoured our music collections and banged together a massive compilation of MP3s. There was only one rule (okay then, two: no death metal), which was that we could only pick one track by each band. This was a tricky business and it took days. How do you narrow down a band such as Deep Purple to one song? The same could apply to Ozzy, AC/DC and Guns N' Roses. It became quite a project, but we were determined to put our stamp on our big day and make it an all-out rock party.

And in this, Santie broadened my view even further. She introduced me to tracks by South African artists I'd never heard of: Mandoza, from Soweto, and ChianoSky from Nelspruit. This wasn't rock or metal of any kind, but that was fine, because, all told, heavy metal is not really a big thing in South Africa. There are a few bands down there, but in terms of radio and TV exposure, it's very thin on the ground. Famous tracks by bands like Bon Jovi, Guns N' Roses, and Europe are clearly familiar to a lot of people, but for the most part heavy metal doesn't make it onto the airwaves. The DJs don't tend to touch it, so in spite of its massive popularity elsewhere in the world, in South Africa metal is a bit of an unknown quantity. It's just the way it is down there.

We also liked the idea of live music, and we knew of a local covers band called The Diversions. We'd seen them playing at Whistle Binkies in Edinburgh, and they were just the ticket. If we could fit in MP3 tracks alongside sets of live music, that would be even better.

*

We picked a hotel venue in Ayrshire and, on the night before the ceremony, the guests started flowing in. Mum and Dad were there of course, as were Andrew and his wife, Jane, along with their kids, Alex and Ben. Rob was there with his German wife, Kerstin. Aunts, uncles and cousins whom I hadn't seen in years poured in, alongside friends and relatives of Santie. Then, the following morning, along with Emmett (remember Emmett? The photographer from the Sky9 gig in Glasgow?) and his business partner Andrew, there were suits, hats, fascinators, kilts, sporrans and the like practically wall to wall. The bar did a good trade.

I had asked Richard to be my best man. This had actually been my plan ever since I'd been best man for him when he had got married back in 2004. At that point in my life any idea of getting married, where I was concerned, felt like a distant and inaccessible dream.

But there I was: a bloke from Derby, about to marry a woman from Johannesburg. Whom I'd met in Scotland. Who would have thought that could have been on my horizon?

Richard's speech was written in a notebook which had a scaly leathery cover. He was quite proud of it. Shortly before the ceremony, he pulled me aside and showed it to me. 'Hey, Phil, check it out!' he said, whilst running his fingers over the binding. 'I chose this specially for your speech. It's got a kind of Necronomicon look about it. Pretty cool, right?'

'You're right about that. Looks like it's coated with dragon scales. Nice one!'

But right then – I honestly couldn't help it – it leapt right into my mind. A Deicide flashback! The riff from 'Dead by Dawn' rammed its way into my head, and then, fortunately, buggered off again. In the circumstances, its departure was quite welcome. 'Dead by Dawn' isn't the kind of earworm you want lurking around when you're about to say 'I do'.

Great riff though!

We were married in a very simple humanist ceremony, and we walked down the aisle together with 'Ten Words' by Joe Satriani as our soundtrack.

*

Richard's speech was wide ranging and covered all sorts of bases. He mentioned a tendency of mine to tuck my metal T-shirts into my jeans. Personally, I've never had a problem with that. He was, however, adamant that it was 'not cool'. He also recounted an incident at a Love/Hate gig, during which I went tear-assing off the stage at full stretch whilst flattening the bass player's microphone stand. Yep. Mea culpa. As you'll have gathered, I have a history of being a nutter at gigs. W.A.S.P. even got a mention. How about *that?*

Ian, the guy who fronted The Diversions, had also asked me if I wanted to play a few tracks with them during the party. Can you guess what my response to that was?

We rehearsed once on the weekend prior to the wedding, and we nailed several numbers.

On the night, he called me up to join the band in three back-to-back tracks: 'Living After Midnight' by Judas Priest, 'Lil' Devil' by The Cult, and 'Paranoid' by Sabbath. And we floored it! The *play it like you mean it* principle shot through once again. Flat-out full-volume shred! It must have looked a little strange in some ways. It's quite unusual to see tracks like that played by a band with a lead guitarist wearing a three-piece suit and a red tie. Polished shoes as well. But that was all fine: Santie and I never said that we wanted to do things conventionally. Far from it. It is nice to chuck the rule book out of the window and just do things your own way.

And the music kept pumping. The Diversions hit it with tracks by Blondie, Tom Petty, Oasis and others, and between sets we had tracks by the likes of Bon Jovi, Europe, Nightwish and ZZ Top. The guests were bouncing around and having the time of their lives, and Santie was spinning like a top!

Then, at the end of the evening, Ian called me up again, and to finish off we blasted out the heaviest, most metallic, most over the top version of 'Five Hundred Miles' by the Proclaimers that has probably ever been devised by man! Unrehearsed!

It wasn't really the setting for a mosh pit. But that didn't matter. A kind of circle-conga erupted in front of us. A rare site indeed!

*

The following morning, Santie and I disappeared to the Isle of Skye for a few days to decompress. As we travelled northwards through the Highlands, we listened to Planet Rock on the radio. It's always good to hear their DJs playing old classics and also to hear newer tracks by younger bands. But as we got up towards the Five Sisters of Kintail, the signal died a sudden death and the rock was silenced. We fiddled around with the radio for a while, and the only station we could get hold of was the Asian Network. So we let it play and listened to a top twenty countdown of current Asian hits. It then struck me that my T-shirt of the day was for Demonic Resurrection, a metal band from Mumbai. Quite fitting as it turned out. Then, as we turned right, having crossed the Skye bridge at Kyle of Lochalsh, the first thing we saw was an Indian restaurant all set up and ready for business. It's great how some of the most unlikely situations can fit perfectly into place.

We spent about a week trolling around in the Cuillin Mountains, clambering around in caves, and staring in awe at the incredible jagged landscapes that surrounded us. This was just what we thrived on, and it gave us the opportunity to get some perspective on what had happened. Our wedding day had been a blast, and it had all taken place so quickly. It felt quite surreal. After months of planning and preparation, all of a sudden, wham! – you're married. Yes, actually *married!* It was a fantastic feeling and, as I frequently tell Santie in so many words, in finding her, I view myself to be 'a very lucky man!'

Bon Jovi	'Someday I'll Be Saturday Night'
Def Leppard	'Photograph'
Europe	'Coast to Coast'
	'Open Your Heart'
Immolation	'When the Jackals Come'
Judas Priest	'Firepower'
	'No Surrender'
Megadeth	'Dystopia'
	'Poisonous Shadows'
Metallica	'Nothing Else Matters'
	'Unforgiven'
Michael Monroe	'Goin' Down with the Ship'
	'Old King's Road'
Uriah Heep	'It's All Been Said'
Vader	'Iron Reign'

Conclusion

As Helloween succinctly put it way back in 1985, 'Heavy Metal (Is The Law)'. A commendable sentiment indeed, but maybe not entirely enforceable. I mean, nobody is going to leap out from behind and slam you into handcuffs if you're not seen listening to *South of Heaven* or *Rust in Peace* in every waking moment. But at the same time, law or no law, it's a pretty damn good guideline. It's one that I've been abiding by since I was about eleven years old.

And it really is a daily thing. I can't recollect the last twenty-four-hour stretch that I went 'metal free'. You could justifiably call it an addiction. I tune in to the metal radio stations, trawl my way through YouTube, sift my CD and MP3 collections, and blast it out of the car window. I simply have to get that fix!

And with good reason. After all, metal unquestionably lays claim to many of the most creative, unusual, and technically proficient musicians to be found in any genre. Just get a load of John Petrucci, Zakk Wylde, Randy Rhoads and Glenn Tipton. But it's easy to merely focus on the guitarists, as I did for quite some time. The engines that fuel these guys, namely the drummers and bass players, are absolutely fundamental. The majority of Iron Maiden's music is written and driven by Steve Harris, their bass player; and Mike Portnoy's drumming is also crucial to the writing of a lot of

Dream Theater's finest epics. Granted, these guys are big names, but quite often drummers, bass guitarists and keyboard players are the unsung and occasionally unseen heroes of these bands.

From the point at which Van Halen gave me my first peek at the possibilities, through my eye-widening introduction to Iron Maiden, and to the massive metallic web which opened up following this, I still stand in utter, utter awe. As far as I'm concerned, the music definitely chose me. I didn't go out looking for something to be into. Metal appeared, grabbed me by the scruff of the neck, and said, 'You boy. Yes, you. Come here! You're *mine!*'

And there's so much to it. The buzz of metal can be located in so many settings. It could be found in the Black Crowes coming on stage at Donington to grace the crowd with a set of 'muthafuckin' rock 'n' roll'. Or it could be Quorthon rasping out '*FIRE!*' during the Bathory track 'Shores in Flames'. Maybe you'll find it in Kirk Hammett's amazingly delicate solo at the start of Metallica's 'Fade to Black', or in Dave Mustaine's rip-roaring explosions during 'Set the World Afire'. You might find it in Bon Scott's lascivious drooling, Alice Cooper's python-wielding antics, or Rob Halford's tooth-loosening screams.

As for me, I like to think that I've made something of a contribution, albeit modest. I never made it in a band (except perhaps in my own head), but playing in Sky9 was unbelievable. Although the band only lasted for about half a dozen gigs, that experience gave me a taste of the scene, which I will never forget. Realistic dreams of becoming a rock star had taken a dive way back, but that said, cranking out old-school heavy metal at my wedding reception was more than I could have hoped for. In short, it was the best gig I could ever have wanted to play. It will be stamped onto my memory, and Santie's too, forever.

So, to all of those bands, be they household names, newcomers on the scene, or maybe the ones that will always lurk in the darker and more shrouded enclaves, I say sincerely: thank you for the music!

Afterword

It was in October 2020, whilst I was drafting the conclusion to this book, that I heard about the tragic passing of Edward Van Halen. This shocking news came as a blow to fans the world over, and it marked the clear ending of an era. His extraordinary playing style was so vital to the development of rock music in the 1980s that, without him, who knows how things would have panned out? I am fortunate enough to have had the privilege (and privilege is the word) of seeing Van Halen on stage in 1993 at the Birmingham NEC. Truly incredible. What a showman!

Farewell Eddie. And happy trails!

Acknowledgements

Since I started writing this book in February 2019, a whole host of people have assisted me in all sorts of ways, often simply through expressing an interest and encouraging me to persevere. Apologies to anyone I may have forgotten…

Malcolm Dome, the music journalist and heavy metal guru (sadly no longer with us) who was very interested in my book.

Andra Hosking and Tim Hatton for doing read-throughs.

Richard Sheehan for doing a great copy-edit and proofreading job.

Andrew McConville for helping me with one or two IT issues I encountered along the way.

All my pals at Edinburgh Castle for your encouragement right from the get-go.

The guys in SKY9: Iain, Paul and John. We had a blast! I would happily do it again!

My brothers Andrew and Rob and also their wives Jane and Kerstin. I can't wait for you to read this! And my niece, Alex, and nephew, Ben. This book might give you a slightly different perspective on your uncle Phil…

Emmett and Andrew, from Wilson McSheffrey Photography, for all the shots of SKY9 in concert, and for the wedding photography. You did an amazing job!

Brian Edworthy of Wolfworx Photography in South Africa for your picture of Santie with Tribal.

Mum and Dad for all your love and support. You have no idea how much I appreciate it.

And finally, to my wonderful wife, Santie. I don't know where I'd be without you. I will love you, always.